D0663406

Glass
of the '50s & '60s
A Collector's Guide

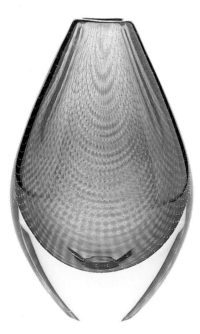

Glass
of the '50s & '60s

A Collector's Guide

Nigel Benson

MILLER'S GLASS OF THE '50S & '60S: A COLLECTOR'S GUIDE
by Nigel Benson

First published in Great Britain in 2002 by Miller's, a division of
Mitchell Beazley, imprints of Octopus Publishing Group Ltd,
2–4 Heron Quays, London E14 4JP

Miller's is a registered trademark of Octopus Publishing Group Ltd

Copyright © Octopus Publishing Group Ltd 2002

Commissioning Editor **Anna Sanderson**
Executive Art Editor **Rhonda Fisher**
Project Editor **Virginia McLeod**
Designer **Louise Griffiths**
Editor **Elizabeth Stubbs**
Proofreader **Joan Porter**
Indexer **Sue Farr**
Picture Research **Giulia Hetherington**
Production **Angela Couchman**
Photography by **Steve Tanner**

All rights reserved. No part of this work may be reproduced or utilized
in any form or by any means, electronic or mechanical, including
photocopying, recording or by any information storage and retrieval
system, without the prior written permission of the publisher.

The publishers will be grateful for any information that will assist them
in keeping future editions up to date. While every care has been taken
in the preparation of this book, the author nor the publisher can accept
any liability for any consequence arising from the use thereof, or the
information contained therein. Values shown should be used as a guide
only as prices vary according to geographical location and demand.

ISBN 1 84000 538 6

A CIP catalogue record for this book is available from the British Library
Set in Bembo, Frutiger and Shannon
Produced by Toppan Printing Co., (HK) Ltd.
Printed and bound in China

Jacket illustrations, front cover, left to right: candle holder by Ronald
Stennet-Willson, Wedgwood, c.1964–68, vase by Art Vannes c.1960s
vase by Ronald Stennet-Willson, Wedgwood, c.1969
Back cover: vase by Per Lutken, Holmegaard, c.1959
Half-title page: "kraka" vase by Sven Palmquist, Orrefors, c.1962
Contents page: vase by Reijmyre, c.1960s

contents

Introduction

There are many areas of 1950s and '60s glass design that are already avidly collected, however, there are still areas that are underrated, and therefore undervalued. This provides an excellent opportunity to collect your favourite glass, whether it be hand-blown one-off pieces, or machine made glass with its stylish appeal. The variety of work illustrated in this book provides an overview to a period of change and diversification in the glass world, coinciding as it did with the boom in post-industrial invention, and the social shifts that placed increasing emphasis on creativity and individuality.

Glass design of this period was heavily influenced by the Scandinavians with the universal appeal of their organic, sculptural forms. Artists at Orrefors and Kosta in Sweden, and Iittala and Nuutajärvi in Finland continued the 20th century design tradition spearheaded by Simon Gate and Edward Hald, and architect Alvar Aalto. The Italians were also influential with their brightly coloured exuberant forms exploring the plasticity

"Occhi" vases, Venini & Co., 1959–1960, **£1500–2200/ $2250–3300** (these vases were reissued in the 1990s, and are valued at £400–600/$600–900)

Textured vase by Geoffrey Baxter, Whitefriars Glassworks, c.1971, ht 15cm/6in, **£50–60/$75–90**

of glass. Vessels were often made purely for decorative purposes in specialist factories, most famously in Murano, near Venice.

In the United States, glass design extended existing pre-war ranges. Particularly notable is Steuben, with their exceptional in-house design team and commissioned artists producing designs for limited edition wares. It was also in America that the revolutionary Studio glass movement was born under the aegis of Harvey Littleton, which had enormously far-reaching effects. In Britain, post-war commercial constraints hindered development, but notable exceptions to the general trend were Whitefriars, with their bias towards form and colour who produced some very stylish wares, and John Luxton, Irene Stevens & David Hammond who continued to promote modern design. The influence of Sam Herman who helped realise the Studio glass movement in England, in the Stourbridge factory, was also beginning to be felt.

Czech glass developed separately from the rest of the world at this time, largely due to the post-war political climate in Eastern Europe. From 1948 the glass industry was combined in one organization under the auspices of the state and included all strands of glass-making. Blown, cut, engraved, and painted glass were incorporated with the educational and technical bodies. Only now, half a century later, are we beginning to fully appreciate the importance of Czech designers of this period.

When starting a collection, establish parameters within which to collect. This will often be stimulated by the first piece you buy. From here, the boundaries can be clarified, and further pieces chosen according to, for example, factory, designer, or country. The advantage of this, is that

'Trees in Fog' vase by Vicke Lindstrand, Kosta, c.1955, ht 32cm/12¹/₂in
£800–1200/ $1200–1800

you can make the most of your resources, even if they are limited. Be aware that except at the most inexpensive end of the market, research and background knowledge are invaluable. Libraries and museums are obvious sources of information. In addition, enlisting a specialist dealer can be beneficial. By definition, these specialists have a particular interest and depth of knowledge which they will usually share with you when you are purchasing a particular item.

When purchasing glass, remember it will not always be possible to find bargains. To avoid the pitfall of a large but unremarkable collection, take a pragmatic view and "average the cost" of your purchases. This will allow you to see the bigger picture of your collection, keep an eye on your expenditure, and give you value for money. It is also advisable to build a collection based on your personal taste, rather than for the potential investment value. As with all investments, a piece of glass can just as easily decrease as increase in value. Whatever the impetus, buy what you like and what gives you the most pleasure.

This book cannot, unfortunately, fully illustrate the extraordinary array of '50s and '60s glass, however, it does provide a useful starting point, as well as presenting some lesser known but deserving work to a new audience. Whatever you choose to collect, this is an area of tremendous diversity, offering endless opportunities to pursue your chosen subject. Collecting may also bring unexpected bonuses, providing an insight into the lifestyles and design influences of the mid-20th century, a prolific, diverse, and fascinating era.

Value of pieces

Prices vary depending on the condition of the piece of glass, its rarity and where it is purchased, so the prices given in this book are an approximate guide only. The sterling/dollar conversion has been made at a rate of £1 = $1.50, but you will need to adjust the dollar value as necessary to accord with current exchange rates.

Blown transparent glass

The basic form used for any blown glass object is a bubble. Initially a gather (or blob) of molten glass is taken from the furnace on the end of a hollow blowing iron. The glassblower then blows it, either freely or into a mould, to the required shape and size, while spinning it to keep it centred. Then it is transferred to a solid pontil iron, at which point the bubble can be opened and shaped using pucellas and shears. Once shaped, it is broken off the iron and left in a cooling oven, or "lear". A wide variety of clear and transparent coloured glass is illustrated here, the style of each object reflecting the precise period in which it was made and its country of origin, although simple, sculptural forms from Scandinavia dominated the post-war era.

◀ **Vase by John Orwar Lake**
Little is known about the Swedish company Ekenås, yet its pieces regularly appear in the marketplace.
The main designer and art director from 1953 until its closure in 1976 was John Orwar Lake (b.1921), a sculptor who had worked in ceramics for the Finnish firm, Arabia. This bulbous vase, with its turnover rim, has an applied band of impressed circular marks around its "neck" in the same colour as the body. The result is a subtle, homogenous design, in a decorative style reminiscent of Danish and Swedish ceramics of the period.

Vase by John Orwar Lake, Ekenås, c.1950s, ht 13cm/5in, **£40–50/ $60–75**

▶ **"Selina" vase by Sven Palmquist**
The subtle pink, opalescent colour and simple, understated organic forms of "Selina" glassware exemplify Swedish design of the 1950s. This range by Sven Palmquist (1906–84) demonstrates his versatility, showing an ability to design for production as well as being able to produce the highly technical "Ravenna" and "Kraka" pieces that took so long to develop (see p.20). "Selina" is one of the many affordable Orrefors wares produced in the 1950s and 1960s and is still available to collectors today.

"Selina" vase by Sven Palmquist, Orrefors, c.1954, ht 25.5cm/10in, **£70–80/$105–120**

FACT FILE

- Damage to free-blown transparent glass is immediately apparent and cannot be camouflaged by textured surfaces or opaque colours. Even scratches may affect the value of an item as they are so visible, especially in a lit display.

Vase by James Hogan, Whitefriars Glassworks, c.1940–48, ht 19.5cm/7¹/₂in, **£40–50/$60–75**

▲ **Vase by James Hogan**
This vase is part of a series designed by James Hogan (1883–1948) between 1940 and 1948, characterized by heavy bases and thick walls. It appears to be a reworking of some pieces designed for Whitefriars by Tom Hill in 1937. Hogan's items, however, are more distinctive and lighter in approach, their "lobed" bases and "tooled" rims separated by a curved panel. While the shape and weight of these pieces make them excellent flower vases, they work equally well as mini-sculptures.

▼ **Vase by Timo Sarpaneva**
Timo Sarpaneva (b.1926), joined Karhula-Iittala in 1950, and this simple, thick-walled asymmetric vase is typical of his early work. One of Finland's most influential designers, Sarpaneva received international recognition when he won both the 1954 and 1957 Milan Triennial Grand Prix and the prestigious Lunning Prize in 1956. Much of his work is extremely expensive, but pieces like this are still obtainable at comparatively moderate prices.

Vase by Timo Sarpaneva, Iittala, c.1956, ht 6.5cm/2¹/₂in, **£120–150/$180–225**

Ashtray by Per Lütken, Holmegaard, c.1955, dia. 13cm/5in, **£24–32/$36–48**

▲ **Ashtray by Per Lütken**
Per Lütken (1916–98) was a prolific designer for the Danish companies Holmegaard and Kastrup, from the time of his appointment as resident designer in 1942, until his death. His awareness of the qualities of glass and his ability to explore its plasticity exhibit a great understanding of his craft. This simple piece shows how his work could be sophisticated even when producing something as functional as an ashtray. While the overall form is symmetrical, the central opening is stylishly offset.

▼ Ruby "ribbon ware" vase by Barnaby Powell

"Ribbon ware" was originally designed by Barnaby Powell (1891–1939) in 1932. The series, with its spiralling applied decoration, was so successful however, that Whitefriars continued to produce it through until the 1960s. The popular "ruby" colour first appeared in the 1940 catalogue, but production of ruby glass did not really start until after World War II and the end of restrictions on luxury glass production. Consequently, ruby glass from this and other series could not have appeared until 1947, making them firmly post-war.

Ruby "ribbon ware" vase by Barnaby Powell, Whitefriars Glassworks, c.1949, ht 13.5cm/ 5¹/₄in, **£25–35/$40–55**

Bowl by Ingeborg Lundin, Orrefors, c.1954, ht 5cm/2in, **£38–48/$60–75**

▲ Bowl by Ingeborg Lundin

At first sight, this bowl appears simple in form. Closer inspection, however, reveals an asymmetric rim, flat and wide on one side and shaped to a curved edge on the other. As a result, Ingeborg Lundin (1921–92) achieves a sculptural quality to what might otherwise be a completely functional item. The piece typifies Scandinavian work of the post-war era, combining as it does, sculptural style with function.

▼ Bowl by Donald Pollard

We usually expect a vase or bowl bought at a department store to have clarity without imperfection. This quality, however, is only achieved by good glass "recipes", or chemistry, and good quality control. Clear glass from the American company Steuben from the 1930s onward, is particularly fine, its clarity augmented by a simplicity of design. This bowl by Donald Pollard (b.1924) explores the natural beauty of glass through its simple form, and is enhanced by the implied movement achieved by adding applied swirls of glass to the base.

Bowl by Donald Pollard, Steuben, c.1960s, **£80–100/$120–150**

▼ Vase by Blenko

This vase, inspired by ancient classical designs, is typical of Blenko's work from between the wars, although this example was actually produced after World War II. The foot is solid, with a ground-out pontil, its shape being one of the features that identify it as Blenko glassware, and were it not for the weighted base, the vase would be physically and aesthetically unbalanced. The factory style was to change dramatically when Winslow Anderson (b.1914) joined in 1947 and introduced Italian and Scandinavian influences.

Vase by Blenko, c.1946, ht 37.5cm/14³/₄in, **£60–80/$90–120**

"Fork" vase by James Hogan, Whitefriars Glassworks, c.1945, ht 23.5cm/9¹/₄in, **£65–80/$100–120**

▲ "Fork" vase by James Hogan

This thick-walled vase, designed by James Hogan (1883–1948) exhibits a fusing of British economy of design with a simple sculptural form that reflects Scandinavian style. These vases were produced in flint, sea-green, sapphire blue, and amber (seen here) which works particularly well with the light refracting through it, bringing the colour to life. The intensity of the colour varies with the thickness of the glass, accentuating the form of the vase.

FACT FILE

• A factory may have a house style, although this may not be immediately apparent. Sometimes it is one particular designer within a factory whose work is most noticeable, or collectable. The use of reference material, is therefore essential for identifying the origin and pedigree of a piece.

▼ Vase by Willy Johansson

The red on the rim of this vase accentuates its shape and the smallness of the opening, giving a lift to the smoky colour of the body, where it merges into it at a carefully prescribed point. Without this detail, the squat barrel shape would still conform to principles of form and function, however, Willy Johansson (1921–93) has produced a vase that transcends this, and is thus typical of Modern Scandinavian style.

Vase by Willy Johansson, Hadeland, c.1950s, ht14.5cm/ 5³/₄in, **£120–140/$180–210**

Blown cased glass

Cased glass is produced by blowing two or more layers of glass together, one of which will usually be clear. It may then be cut, etched, engraved, or decorated with applied designs. During the post-war era, much of this type of glass came from Scandinavia, and the heavily clear-cased work had a major influence on international glass design. Cased glass of this period ranges from the expensive Scandinavian masterpieces, such as "ariel" or "graal" glass and the "Ravenna" and "Kraka" series (see p.20), to more affordable pieces which often include streaky or trapped bubble decoration (see p.18). Some of the less-collected, good quality cased glassware was produced by companies such as Åfors, Flygfors, Maastricht, and Strömbergshyttan. Much British cased glass from the 1950s was rather overlooked until recently.

Vase by Vicke Lindstrand, Kosta, c.1955, ht 13.5cm/5³/₄in, **£120–140/$180–210**

▶ **Vase by Vicke Lindstrand**
This simply shaped vase is part of versatile designer Vicke Lindstrand's (1904–83) large body of work for Kosta. The single dark amethyst line is designed to complement the form of the vase, outlining its shape. This hot-blown vase represents the affordable end of Lindstrand's work for today's collector. Beware of scuffed or scratched pieces, since it is the clarity of Swedish glass in particular that is an essential part of the design.

▼ **"Knobberly" Bowl by W. Wilson & H. Dyer**
The "Knobberly" range was developed by William Wilson (1914–72), chief designer and managing director of Whitefriars, and glass-blower Harry Dyer. The shapes and colours for the two ranges, one in clear glass with random streaks, the other in solid colour, were produced by twisting or pulling the gather prior to blowing out.

'Knobberly' bowl by W. Wilson & H. Dyer, Whitefriars Glassworks, c.1964, dia. 21.5cm/8¹/₂in, **£45–55/$70–85**

• Work by
Scandinavian designers
such as Hald, Lindstrand
and Palmquist, and
Italians including A.
Barbini, E. Barovier, N.
Martinuzzi, F. Poli, and
particularly Paolo Venini,
and A.D. Copier for
Leerdam in Holland is all
important and sought
after by collectors.

FACT FILE

▼ Vase by Ronald Stennet-Willson

Here, a range of coloured enamels has been rolled into the gather before being cased and blown, producing an opaque effect. Ronald Stennet-Willson (b.1916) has carefully limited the range of complementary colours to create a cohesive work. He was clearly influenced by Scandinavian glass design of the 1950s and 1960s, but his work has a distinctly British slant, seen here in the bold symmetrical shape.

Vase by Ronald Stennet-Willson, Wedgwood, c.1969, ht 12cm/4³/₄in, **£30–40/$45–60**

Bowl by Willy Johansson, Hadeland, c.1955, dia. 25.5cm/10in, **£70–80/$105–120**

▲ Bowl by Willy Johansson

Here Willy Johansson (1921–93) has transformed an otherwise ordinary transparent grey bowl, adding a vertical rim by extending the clear casing. To exaggerate the effect, he has then included spiralling black lines within the rim. Contrasting colours was an effect Johansson explored throughout much of his work and the inclusion of spiralling opaque enamels was also a favoured technique.

Vase by Per Lütken, Holmgaard, c.1959, ht 10cm/4in, **£40–50/$60–75**

▲ Vase by Per Lütken

Per Lütken (1916–98) is well known for the fluid forms he produced in the 1950s, in which he exploits the plasticity of the material using pulling and twisting techniques. This vase, however, is an example of his more restrained work of the period, and demonstrates how he worked equally well in cased coloured glass. The vase was available in different sizes, and has an incised mark on its base with Lütken's monogram.

Vase by William Wilson,
Whitefriars Glassworks, c.1954,
ht 14.5cm/5¹/₂in,
£25–32/$40–50

▲ Vase by William Wilson
Sometimes referred to as
"tooth" vases because of their
resemblance to molars, these
lobed vases acknowledge the
influence of Scandinavian
glass in their overall design.
Both the organic form and the
use of heavy casing are traits
of this influence, although
there is also a continuity that
reflects the Whitefriars
inheritance – note the lobed
vases by James Hogan (see
p.9). Wilson (1914–72) is
recognized as promoting the
use of strong colours,
complementing the usual
Whitefriars tradition of a
subtle colouration that
enhanced the limpid look
of their wares.

**▼ "Coquille" vase
by Paul Kedelv**
"Coquille" was a successful
range, originally based on
shells, produced by the
Swedish company Flygfors
during the 50s and 60s.
Designed by Paul Kedelv
(b.1917) and master-blower
Fritz Ek, the pieces range from
gentle curved sculptural forms
through to highly sculpted
vessels with pulled rims, such
as the piece below. Although
Flygfors produced quality
work, it has been overlooked
by collectors who have until
recently favoured the more
recognized Swedish companies.

"Coquille" vase by Paul Kedelv,
Flygfors, c.1957, ht 27cm/10¹/₂in,
£60–70/$90–105

"Harrtil" ashtray by Milan
Metelák & Milos Pulpitel,
Harrachev Glassworks,
Czechoslovakia (Czech Republic)
c.1955, ht 5.5cm/2¹/₄in,
£35–45/$55–70

**▲ "Harrtil" ashtray by
M. Metelák & M. Pulpitel**
"Harrtil" glassware was
designed by Milan Metelák
(b.1928) and Harrachev
Glassworks manager Milos
Pulpitel in 1955. The fine
white mesh of woven glass
fibres trapped within a heavy
casing can be seen in all the
pieces in the series. The
random band of colour in this
ashtray is, however, more
unusual. These pieces have
often been mistaken for Italian
glassware because of
similarities in form and colour,
however their restrained
organic forms and rigid mesh-
like decoration set them apart.

Vase by Floris Meydam, Leerdam, c.1950s, ht 16cm/6^1/$_4$in, **£150–180/$225–270**

▲ Vase by Floris Meydam

This piece by Floris Meydam (b.1919), for the Netherlands company Leerdam, is typical of his work from the 1950s, with its gently organic form and vivid cased colour. The flattened form teeters between symmetric and asymmetric, producing a carefully balanced organic quality. The clear wings exaggerate the underlay of blue, and Meydam has also cleverly allowed the top area of blue to spread into the wings, giving movement to what might otherwise have become a static design. Work by Meydam is increasing in value, however pieces are still affordable for many collectors.

▼ "Dusk Ware" vase by Nils Landberg

Most of the pieces from the "Dusk" series by Nils Landberg (1907–91) are organic in form, with a thick casing over an underlay of muted green or grey, the colour accentuating the shape of the piece. Many had an angular elliptical section, or flattened diamond shape, demonstrating Landberg's feeling for form and his awareness of the pliability of glass. Two of the shapes, a tall triangular and a flattened bottle form, reflect his particular flair for attenuated form.

"Dusk Ware" vase by Nils Landberg, Orrefors, c.1955–57, ht 18.5cm/7^1/$_4$in, **£65–75/$100–115**

FACT FILE

- Many European factories mark their work with incised inscriptions. Learn the marks of the factory or designer you wish to collect, but be aware that it is possible to imitate these marks.
- Cased ware from this period is generally accessible and affordable, although unique pieces are far more expensive.

Vase by Max Verboeket, Maastricht, c.1955, ht 21cm/8^1/$_4$in, **£80–90/$120–135**

▲ Vase by Max Verboeket

This vase was part of a popular series by Max Verboeket (b.1922), an artist, and chief designer for Netherlands company Maastricht Kristalunie in the mid-1950s, and was produced for around twenty years. The thick-walled pieces were free blown, and manipulated into shape while hot, often into exaggerated forms with "spines" running from base to rim. In each piece, two coloured streaks are wisped randomly through the body.

Art glass & studio glass

Studio-based glass was produced throughout the 1920s and 1930s, but by World War II its popularity was on the wane, and many companies were forced to close. Some wares continued to be produced in Britain by factories such as Monart, Nazeing, and the new Ysart Bros., but by 1962 a new hot-blown studio glass movement was emerging from the USA under the guidance of Harvey Littleton (*b*.1922). A revolutionary low temperature formula for hot-blown glass, developed by Dominic Labino, allowed artists to create work independently of the commercial companies. A lecture by Littleton at the RCA in 1967 kick-started the movement in Britain, but it did not really get underway until Sam Herman opened The Glasshouse studio in London in 1969.

▼ **Vase by Sam Herman**
Sam Herman (*b*.1936), a Mexican-born American, was one of the most influential figures in modern hot-glass blowing in Britain. He completed his post-graduate studies at the RCA in London, and was made tutor of the glass department between 1969 and 1974. Herman believed in spontaneous design and took advantage of the fact that preconceived designs could be changed while actually blowing. His vibrant pieces range in colour from the subdued (such as this bottle vase) through to bright oranges and reds, often with random iridized swirls.

Vase by Sam Herman, 1971, ht 17cm/6³/₄in, **£150–180/ $225–270**

▶ **Vase by Strathearn**
Strathearn Glass was formed in 1965 after Teacher's Whisky became a major shareholder in Vasart. Much of its output was a continuation of the Vasart style, and one range (shown here) was very similar to Monart Glass. This range was made in a single colour-way of black and aventurine (as in this vase), occasionally with darker swirls of the base colour. Strathearn items, however, can usually be distinguished from Monart and Vasart wares by their comparative weightiness, their thicker, glossier casing, and by the impressed Strathearn mark on their bases.

Vase by Strathearn, 1965–71, ht 20cm/7³/₄in, **£75–85/ $115–130**

Bowl & ashtray by Nazeing, c.1950s, dia. 20cm/7³/₄in (bowl), ht 4.5cm/1³/₄in (ashtray), **£30–40/$45–60 (bowl), £18–25/$30–40 (ashtray)**

▲ Bowl & ashtray by Nazeing

In the years immediately following World War II, Nazeing continued to produce many of their pre-war shapes, such as the bowl shown here. The colours in which they were produced, however, changed considerably, probably because glass factories could no longer buy the enamels they had originally used from their old sources. After the war, Nazeing also began to employ a heavy clear base in some of its coloured glassware, such as this ashtray. Both pre- and post-war pieces are both affordable and readily available.

▼ Vases by Vasart

Vasart glass was made in Scotland by Salvador Ysart (1887–1956) and his two sons Augustine and Vincent, and was similar to wares produced by their former employer, John Moncrieff Ltd. Vasart favoured muted shades, and had a comparatively limited range of shapes. They produced inexpensive pieces such as these vases, as well as bowls, fruit sets and lamps, often with wavy edges.

Vases by Vasart, 1947, (left to right) ht 18.5cm/7¹/₄in, ht 9cm/3³/₄in, ht 6cm/2¹/₂in, **£80–110/$120–165 (left), £20–30/$30–45 (others)**

FACT FILE

- Most hand-blown work by individual artists can be identified by an inscribed signature, often accompanied by the date, while factory pieces usually have labels.
- Labels can be washed off or worn away and signatures can be faked – so it is important to familiarize yourself with the style and construction of the work you propose to collect.

Vase by Mdina, c.1968, ht 35cm/13³/₄in, **£40–50/$60–75**

▶ Vase by Mdina

After five years as a tutor at the RCA in London, Michael Harris (1933–94) left Britain in 1967 to set up Mdina Glass in Malta. With him went Italian glass-blowers, Vicente and Ettore Boffo, who not only produced the new glass, but also trained apprentices on an island with no tradition of glass-blowing. The resulting glassware, inspired by the colours of the coast and the sea, uses aqua blues, greens, sandy ochres, and browns.

Blown bubbled glass

Trapped air bubbles have been used in glass production throughout the 20th century. Maurice Marinot (1882–1960) and his followers all exploited random bubble decoration, as did the factories of Leerdam, Monart, Nazeing and Schneider between the wars. However, it was the Scandinavians who used bubbles in controlled, symmetrical patterns to greatest effect. With the introduction of "ariel" glass by Orrefors in 1937, trapped bubbles were used to define the subjects within stylized figurative pieces. Other special techniques such as "kraka", "ravenna", and "graal" glass, introduced in the '30s and '40s, can also be included as forms of bubbled glass decoration (see p.20). In the 1960s geometric patterns and simplified forms that were typical of this decade came to the fore.

"Gauze" bowl by Kaj Franck,
Nuutäjarvi Notsjö, c.1953,
dia. 12.5cm/5in,
**£240–280/
$360–420**

▶ **"Gauze" bowl
by Kaj Franck**
Kaj Franck's
(1911–89) periodic
exploration of bubble
decoration usually
resulted in random bubble
effects such as in the
"Sargasso" series of 1966. In
this bowl, however, his
approach is more disciplined,
and the pattern is formed by
fine, controlled bubbles on a
diagonal, alternating with a
pale stripe. The resulting
ghostly haze may well have
been inspired by mist or
cloud, since much Finnish
work of this period took
nature as its theme.

"Flair"bowl by David Hammond
& Stanley Everson, Thomas
Webb & Sons, c.1961,
l. 34cm/13½in,
£60–70/$90–105

▼ **"Flair" bowl by David
Hammond & Stanley Everson**
This series, by Thomas Webb's
chief designer David
Hammond (b.1931) and the
technical director, Stanley
Everson, reflects the influence
of 1950s Scandinavian glass in
its thick walls and sculptural
forms. They were decorated in
a variety of colours, and
embellished with trapped
bubbles within a heavy casing.
Some pieces are asymmetrical,
an effect achieved by pulling
and contorting both the
coloured decoration and body
of the vessel.

▼ Vase by Geoffrey Baxter

Geoffrey Baxter (1926–95) designed this series between 1954 and 1957 at a time when various companies were producing similar bucket-shaped and curved-sided vases with bubble decoration. What distinguishes this piece is the simple device of the pulled-up rim. It also demonstrates Baxter's familiarity with the plasticity of glass, and of organic Scandinavian designs. Up until this point, Whitefriars usually used transparent colours, so the thickly-cased strong colour used here marks a notable change in direction.

Vase by Geoffrey Baxter, Whitefriars Glassworks, c.1955, ht 11cm/4¼in, **£40–50/$60–75**

Vase by Vicke Lindstrand, Kosta, c.1955, ht 18cm/7in, **£100–120/$150–180**

▲ Vase by Vicke Lindstrand

The prolific designer Vicke Lindstrand (1904–83) joined the Kosta factory in 1950, having previously worked for Orrefors. Much of his work is beautifully sculptural and often relies on linear patterns within the glass for decoration. In this elegant, restrained vase, the colour is bold, and the usual line pattern is replaced by a controlled pattern of bubbles. These stand out against the dark background and refract the light like jewelled pearls.

FACT FILE

• Look out for flattened areas on what should be a curved surface, as these may suggest that the item has been repaired. Like abrasions or chips, repair work can considerably devalue an item, often rendering it worthless.
• Badly distorted or out of line bubbles may indicate that the piece was originally a second.

▼ Vase by Gunnel Nyman

During her short career, Gunnel Nyman (1909–48) created many influential pieces to worldwide acclaim, and her use of bubbles was often imitated. Patterns of tiny, symmetrically placed bubbles can be seen in both her clear and coloured pieces. In these latter items, including this vase, the colour was cased prior to the addition of the bubble decoration and then a heavy outer casing.

Vase by Gunnel Nyman, Nuutäjarvi Notsjö, 1947, ht 31cm/12¼in, **£180–220/ $270–330**

Special techniques

Although "ariel" and "graal" techniques were employed by other companies, it was the versatile and innovative Orrefors who introduced both types of glass, and subsequently produced "slip-graal", "kraka", and "Ravenna", progressively through the 1940s. Orrefors designers Edward Hald (1883–1980), Vicke Lindstrand (1904–83), and Sven Palmquist (1906–84), were all aware of the pioneering work of Maurice Marinot (1882–1960) of France, and Andries Dirk Copier (1901–91) of Leerdam Glassworks, in Holland, and strove to develop the "graal" technique into a modern idiom. All these techniques were ground-breaking when they were introduced, and confirmed Orrefors as a world leader in glass production. They are all still highly prized by collectors today.

"Kraka" vase by Sven Palmquist, Orrefors, c.1962, ht 17cm/6³/₄in, **£380–450/ $570–675**

▼ **"Kraka" vase by Sven Palmquist**
The prolific and inspired Orrefors designer, Sven Palmquist (1906–84) invented the "kraka" process in 1944. It is a development of the "graal" technique and produces an extremely delicate net-like pattern. The item is formed by sandblasting a blank covered with a fine mesh. After re-heating, the piece is clear-cased and blown into shape, revealing a net-like pattern of trapped air bubbles. The series derives its name from a Nordic legend in which a beautiful woman, Kraka, agrees to visit a Viking hero "neither dressed, nor undressed", and so she arrives draped in a fish net.

▲ **"Slip-Graal" bowl by Edward Hald**
"Slip-graal", or "cut graal", which is a variation of the "graal" technique, first appeared in 1940, although most was made after World War II. Much of it, like this bowl by Edward Hald, was decorated with lines, stripes, checks, or diagonals, and occasionally with circles. The simple finished style disguises the complexity of this technique.

'Slip-Graal' bowl by Edward Hald, Orrefors, c.1955, dia. 10cm/4in, **£150–180/ $225–270**

- These pieces all represent technical mastery in glass-making. Earlier pieces in any series tend to be expensive, so look for later items that were produced through into the 1980s. Quality versions of "graal" or "ariel" from factories other than Orrefors are good buys.

"Ravenna" bowl by Sven Palmquist, Orrefors, c.1955, dia. 28cm/11in, **£1800–2200/$2700–3300**

▲ **"Ravenna" bowl by Sven Palmquist**

The "Ravenna" series came into being when Sven Palmquist was inspired by French stained glass and the mosaics of Ravenna, in Italy. The glass is made by sandwiching together and then flattening a thick clear layer of glass with a coloured layer. These are then cooled, and a pattern is sandblasted through the colour, and powdered coloured enamels scattered into its recesses. After reheating, molten clear glass is then used to seal the decoration before the piece is returned to the furnace, prior to shaping. These pieces were expensive to produce, and are much prized by collectors.

▼ **"Ariel" bowl by Edvin Örmstrom**

Edvin Örmstrom (1906–94), one of the leading exponents of "ariel" glass at Orrefors, is famous for both his figurative thick-walled coloured pieces, and the transparent pieces with watery figures, both produced in the 1930s. These pieces are prohibitively expensive for most collectors, however, some of the thick-walled pieces were later reproduced and are more affordable. The simple patterned items he made in the 1960s, including the striped "ariel" bowl shown here are also accessible and affordable.

"Ariel" bowl by Edvin Örmstrom, Orrefors, c.1960s, dia. 14cm/5$^{1/2}$in, **£180–220/$270–330**

"Graal" vase by Willem G. de Moor, Flygfors, c.1950, ht 15cm/6in, **£350–400/$525–600**

▲ **"Graal" vase by Willem G. de Moor**

Although Orrefors dominated "graal" glass production during the 1950s, Flygfors, another Swedish company, was also producing it. Willem G. de Moor, Flygfors' first art director, designed this heavy "Flying Geese" "graal" vase which amply illustrates the comany's technical capabilities. This piece would generally command a lower price than a similar Orrefors "graal" piece, and is thus good value for money.

Italian glass

The post-war years saw an explosion of vibrant colour and fantastic form in Italian glass-making, notably from the island of Murano, near Venice, which has been the centre of Venetian glass making for centuries. This flare for colour and complex design built upon the influential work of Barovier & Toso, and Venini from between the wars, and the work of designers such as Dino Martens (1894–1970), Fulvio Bianconi (1915–96), and Flavio Poli (1900–84) is now highly sought after, and therefore expensive. However, it is possible to buy less expensive items by known designers and companies, particularly later pieces from ranges that were produced for long periods (see Occhi vases p.6). It is also possible to build a good representative collection of non-designer wares or work by lesser-known companies.

Murano pitcher, c.1950s,
ht 27.5cm/10³/₄in,
£50–60/$75–90

▶ **Murano pitcher**
The shape of this pitcher, with its pulled-out rim forming a rudimentary handle and its beaked spout, is typically Italian. It was a popular form with several of the major designers of the period, and its heavy vertical ribbing is also very characteristic of 1950s Italian design. The halo effect of the amber line casing the original gather of green, together with the clear outer casing, is referred to as "sommerso" (see p.38).

▼ **Murano bowl**
The colour combination and green "blob" decoration of this bowl could only be Italian, and from this period. The practice of using contrasting colours was a common one, although brighter combinations were more usual. The bowl's organic form and exploitation of the plasticity of glass is also typically Italian. For the collector, pieces of this kind offer a period look on a budget.

Murano bowl, 1950s,
l. 17cm/6³/₄in, **£30–40/$45–60**

- Italian glass is a minefield for collectors who want specific items, as so many companies were influenced by or copied each other. Later copies of important works are also known. If you wish to buy at the top end of the range, research is essential, and the assistance of a knowledgeable specialized dealer advisable.

▼ Murano glass egg

Venini & Co. produced a commercially successful range of large glass eggs during the 1950s, and in this example an unidentified Murano glassworks has imitated their success. This piece, with its randomly veined, cased, yellow base colour, takes its decorative influence from polished semi-precious stones and rock strata. It is a less expensive alternative to Venini.

Murano glass egg, c.1950s, ht 15.5cm/6in, **£50–65/$75–100**

Murano Bowl, c.1950s, dia. 17.5cm/6³/₄in, **£80–100/$120–150**

▲ Murano bowl

Stylistically, this bowl bears a great resemblance to the work of Dino Martens (1894–1970) who worked for Aureliano Toso, becoming the company's artistic director in 1947. Both the elliptical form and the spiralled bands of colour alternated with fine golden lines are characteristic of his work. In this case, these similarities are not enough to make a conclusive attribution, which probably indicates that the bowl is a derivative piece from one of the many Murano factories. Getting the attribution right is vital, since the work of major Italian glass designers can command very high prices.

▶ Murano decanter

Although this decanter lacks the spontaneity of a designer piece, its general style is typical of Italian glassware of the period. Its stretched neck defies logic to achieve a balance of proportion between the large stopper and the base. The stopper does not fit snugly, a deliberate money-saving production technique, as the decanter was probably only ever intended for decorative use.

Murano decanter, c.1950s–60s, **£60–70/ $90–105**

Murano vase, 1960s,
ht 19cm/7¹/₂in,
£50–60/$75–90

▲ Murano vase

The eye-catching colour combination used in this vase suitably enhances its subtle form. The coloured stripes bear a strong resemblance to the decorative style evident in the "Spicchi" series designed by Fulvio Bianconi (1915–96) for Venini, however, it lacks the acid-etched Venini mark. Such unmarked pieces can be confusing to the collector, although inexpensive pieces executed by less well-known glassworks or designers offer considerable style and value for money.

▼ "Lenti" vase by Ercole Barovier

Not all Italian glass was brightly coloured, as can be seen in this clear "Lenti" vase. Its heavy nodular decoration is typical of much of the mid-century work by Ercole Barovier (1889–1974). Designed in the 1940s, these clear pieces were probably not available until the 1950s, due to the intervention of World War II. Here Barovier decorates the entire surface of the vase with a heavy relief, the nodules allowing light to refract through the glass.

"Lenti" vase by Ercole Barovier, Barovier & Toso, c.1940, ht 28cm/11in, **£280–350/$420–525**

Vase by Luciano Gaspari, Salviati & Co., c.1966, ht 33.5cm/13in, **£240–280/$360–420**

▲ Vase by Luciano Gaspari

Much of the glassware designed by Luciano Gaspari (b.1913) for Salviati included the application of extra glass to the surface of the vessel, either to exaggerate its form, or, as here, purely for decoration. Despite its subtle transparent body colour, without its band of decorative applied coloured roundels, this vase would be a purely functional item. Instead, it is given a lift by a playful design that reflects Gaspari's awareness of Pop Art.

FACT FILE

• Work by the Italian factory Venini & Co. can be identified and dated by marks to the base, which, during the 1950s and '60s, took the form of acid-etched marks.
• Many of the other major factories and designers only used labels which are now usually missing.

▼ **Egg timer**
by Paolo Venini

Juxtaposing bright colours is a typically Italian theme, used here to enliven an otherwise utilitarian object. It was designed by Paolo Venini (1895–1959) during the Pop Art era, and its vivid colours echo the style of that movement. Fusing two colours with such precision requires great concentration and illustrates the skill of the blower. This is one of the more affordable Venini items available today.

Egg timer by Paolo Venini, Venini & Co., c.1960s, ht 19cm/7¹/₂in, **£150–180/$225–270**

Murano bowl, c.1950s, l. 36cm/14in, **£60–80/$90–120**

▲ **Murano Bowl**

This thick-walled, boat-shaped bowl has been skillfully made and has a stylish look that would complement many collections. The colour scheme is reminiscent of the world-renowned "Valve" vases designed by Flavio Poli (1900–84) for Seguso. Yet despite its fluid shape, its weight and thick casing indicate that it is unlikely to be from that series of simple, shell-like organic forms. It is typical of the many derivative wares made by Murano factories during this period.

"Inciso" vase by Paolo Venini, Venini & Co, c.1955, ht 21.5cm/8¹/₂in, **£580–650/$870–975**

▼ **"Inciso" vase**
by Paolo Venini

This vase by Paolo Venini is more sophisticated than similar works using the "sommerso" technique. Its outer surface has been worked with a pattern of shallow incised cuts which give the range its name. This textured pattern diffuses the colour and produces a surface effect that could not be achieved by acid-etching alone, as this would only have produced a flat, satin finish. The pattern, made from groups of shallow cuts, are randomly directional, so that light hitting the surface of the glass softens the look of the piece.

Mould-blown glass

Mould-blown glass can be machine-made or, as in most of the pieces shown in this section, free-blown into a mould by a glass-blower. The advantages of using a mould are consistency of shape, size, and quality. Many factories used moulds to assist production, with hand finishing used to achieve a free-blown, and thus more expensive look to their wares. Commercial competition was constantly improving the standard of glass design during the 1950s and 1960s, and as glass manufacturers vied for customers, many handsome ranges were produced. Indeed it is sometimes easy to forget that many of these objects were made as utilitarian wares. Today, collectors are reappraising mould-blown glass, and it is becoming increasingly popular, particularly work that represents iconic styles of the period.

◀ **Vase by Riihimäki Glassworks**

This self-coloured, red vase is part of a large series of wares produced by Finland's Riihimäki Glassworks in the late 1960s. In Britain, this range is known as "Lasi" glass (see p.35) after the maker's full title Riihimäen Lasi Oy (Riihimäen Glass Company). There is no conclusive evidence with which to identify the designer of this particular vase. Its bright red colour was popular in the post-war period, and, with its Pop Art overtones, well suited to the décor of the late 1960s.

Vase by Riihimäki Glassworks, c.1969, ht 24cm/9¹/₂in, **£30–35/$45–55**

▶ **Vase by Per Lütken**

This mould-blown vase was one of a group of three popular vases, originally designed by Per Lütken in the late 1950s, that continued to be produced throughout the 1960s and into the 1970s in differing shapes and colours (not all by Lütken). The vase represents one of the more formalized symmetrical shapes produced by Lütken in the 1950s, at a time when much of his work explored the ductility of glass.

Vase by Per Lütken, Holmegaard, c.1958, ht 13cm/5in, **£40–50/ $60–75**

Vase by Ronald Stennet-Willson, Kings Lynn Glass, c.1967, ht 16.5cm/6½in, **£35–45/$55–70**

▲ Vase by Ronald Stennet-Willson

This vase is an adaptation of a thin-blown floor vase first designed by Stennet-Willson for Lemington Glass in about 1959. It is relatively heavy for its size, having thicker walls than the earlier design, and is far more useful for flower arranging. It was available in transparent coloured, bubbled, or opaque decorated versions, and continued to be produced after Wedgwood bought Kings Lynn in 1969.

▼ "Angular" vase by Geoffrey Baxter

The thin-blown "Angular" series was a modern, harmonious range produced by Whitefriars from designs by Geoffrey Baxter and W. J. Wilson that were based on an old stock of lighting moulds. This clever adaptation still contains hints of the original design's purpose. Although Scandinavian in style, they have a very English restraint, a combination that became very popular when they were produced in the 1960s.

"Angular" vase by Geoffrey Baxter, Whitefriars Glassworks, c.1961, ht 18.5cm/7¼in, **£38–45/$60–70**

FACT FILE

● Moulds are used to give an item its form, and depending on how complex the form to be produced, or how deep any relief decoration is required to be, they can be made of as many as three or four parts.

● Mould-blown wares have recently begun to be noticed by collectors, making it an area of much possibility.

Vase by Kaj Franck, Nuutäjarvi Notsjö, c.1962, ht 25cm/9¾in, **£150–180/ $225–270**

◄ Vase by Kaj Franck

This simplified form by Kaj Franck was specifically designed to be shaped by blowing the cased glass into a mould, in order to achieve consistency of production. It is part of a range of glassware that exemplifies Franck's reductive style. Its simple, strong shape is enhanced by thick walls and lifted by the thick clear casing at its base. Incised factory and designer marks are to be found on the underside of the base.

▼ Vase by Domhnall O'Broin

This series was the first range produced by Caithness Glass, and this "heather"-coloured "bowl-vase" by Domhnall O'Broin (b.1934) is a typical example, and one of the more interesting forms of that series. The range was mainly made up of vases, but also included bowls and two lamp bases which were variants of this piece. All were produced by blowing a coloured gather cased in clear glass into a mould, a production technique which ensured uniformity of shape, finish and quality.

Vase by Domhnall O'Broin, Caithness Glass, c.1966, ht 18cm/7in, **£30–40/$45–60**

Vase by Blenko, c.1960s, **£60–70/$90–105**

▲ Vase by Blenko

The opaque orange effect of this vase was achieved by surrounding a first gather of white in an orange casing. The body of the vase was mould-blown, while its neck was shaped by the blower when "working" the vessel. Its bright colour is typical of the Pop Art era, when furniture, textiles, ceramics, and glass styles reflected trends in the art world. This Blenko ware could be mistaken for Holmegaard's "Carnaby" range (see p.35), however, subtle differences in the form and surface texture mark them apart.

▼ Vase by Tamara Aladin

This mould-blown cased vase is part of a series designed by Tamara Aladin (b.1932). Its distinctive simplicity reflects the Scandinavian Modern style, but also appears to owe something to Modernist philosophies of form and function with its minimalist flange and contoured decoration. All the vases in this series are made up of a transparent coloured underlay in amethyst, blue, or brown, with a clear casing and heavy base. The smoothness of the surface is achieved by turning the glass during blowing.

Vase by Tamara Aladin, Riihimäki Glassworks, c.1960s, **£30–40/$45–60**

Vase by Art Vannes, c.1960s, dia. 14cm/5¹/₂in, **£50–60/$90–110**

▲ **Vase by Art Vannes**
Art Vannes preferred the use of clear crystal glass – glass with a high lead content – and in doing so, followed the same post-war trend as other French companies such as Baccarat, Daum, and Sevrés. All produced heavy clear glassware that explored the pliability of the material. Although this vase has been mould-blown, and thus lacks the pulled quality of Daum and Sèvres glass, it conveys the same feel through its lobed, or nodular, form. Other pieces by Art Vannes include figurative subjects, often animals and birds, some of which were produced well into the 1990s.

▼ **Vases by Nanny Still**
These stretched, cylindrical bottle vases were designed in the late 1950s and were popular throughout the 1960s. As a result of the long production run, they are more readily available to collectors today than some other examples of work by Nanny Still (b.1926). They were produced in a variety of colours, including different shades of blue, green, and grey, and look particularly impressive when displayed in a group.

Vases by Nanny Still, Riihimäki Glassworks, c.1958, ht 34cm/13¹/₄in (left) 32cm/12¹/₂in (right), **£90–110/$135–165**

● Mould-blown glass was modestly priced at the time of origination, and generally remains so. Therefore it is important that these pieces are in good condition since any visible damage will significantly devalue them.

FACT FILE

Vase by Per Lütken, Holmegaard, c.1960s, ht 18cm/7in, **£80–100/$120–150**

▲ **Vase by Per Lütken**
This heavy, cylindrical vase is given a lift by the addition of internal spiralling bands of colour. Although heavier, it is very similar to his bottle vase on p.26. In both, simple devices – the internal decoration of this vase and the bottle vase's flat wide rim – completely transform otherwise plain designs.

Mould-blown textured glass

Textured glass became fashionable for about twenty years from the late 1960s. Although its introduction in the mid-1960s is usually credited to Finnish designers, some believe it was introduced independently to Britain through Geoffrey Baxter's designs for Whitefriars. Although similar in concept, Baxter's designs had a totally different approach, and there is evidence that he saw an exhibition of Finnish work in London only after his own first textured series had been launched. Much Finnish textured glass from this period, and some of Geoffrey Baxter's work, is expensive, but both can still be found at reasonable prices, as can work from other countries and designers. As ever, underrated but good quality work from sources other than the mainstream, may be found at very good prices.

Vase by Pukeberg, c.1960s,
ht 11cm/4¼in,
£20–30/$30–45

▶ Vase by Pukeberg
This "solifleur", or single flower vase is typical of the work of the three designers working for Pukeberg between 1957 and 1973. Dating from the late 1960s, it has a fashionable textured surface, but is far more abstract in design than many of its contemporaries. Its geometric form and decoration demonstrate an awareness of the work of major artists and sculptors of the period. In Britain, "Troika" pottery used a similar design theme, reminiscent of the work of artist Ben Nicholson.

▼ "Finlandia" vase by Timo Sarpaneva
The "Finlandia" series, which included vases, bowls, and sculptures, was made by Timo Sarpaneva (b.1926), using wooden moulds that produced textures resembling ice and bark. Each piece was unique; the mould was scorched every time it was used, and the resulting charred surface gave a different textural effect to the next piece blown. This gave a spontaneity to the production of these wares which is not evident in the more available and less valuable production versions of the series.

"Finlandia" vase by Timo Sarpaneva, Iittala, c.1964, 14cm/5½in,
£120–140/ $180–210

▼ Vase by Lars Hellsten

This mould-blown vase by Lars Hellsten (b.1933) for the Swedish firm Skrufs, is far crisper than its press-moulded equivalent. It is architectural in style, its scroll-like decoration reminiscent of classical columns, contrasted against its cut and polished rim, and flat neck and base. It is also more formalized than his spontaneous larger pieces, which have a feeling of free expression, despite being produced by the same method. Hellsten moved to Orrefors in 1972 at a time of great uncertainty in the Swedish glass industry, taking with him his techniques of casting in aluminium or iron moulds.

Vase by Lars Hellsten, Skrufs, c.1960, ht 17cm/6³/₄in, **£70–80/$105–120**

"Pinus" vase by Tapio Wirkkala, Iittala, c.1960, ht 17cm/6³/₄in, **£65–75/$100–115**

▲ "Pinus" vase by Tapio Wirkkala

This ice-like vase by Tapio Wirkkala (1915–85) is part of a production series made by Iittala for a number of years. Its subject matter is typically Finnish, being drawn from the natural world; ice and wood being particular favourites. Unlike British textured wares which tended to be brightly coloured, Finnish textured glass of this period was mostly clear or grey. Some of the pieces in this series have a full incised mark which includes Wirkkala's name and the serial number of the piece; others bear only his initials, or have no mark at all.

FACT FILE

- It is difficult to repair surfaces that have been damaged, so look for polished or flattened areas that do not conform to the surrounding surface texture before purchasing a piece.

▼ "Drunken Bricklayer" vase by Geoffrey Baxter

The wonderful asymmetry of this piece represents a huge leap in style by Whitefriars. In earlier work in this series, Geoffrey Baxter drew on nature for inspiration (see p.32), however, here he is inspired by man-made objects. The textured surface of the panels are produced by the carpet tacks nailed into the wooden mould leaving localised impressions.

"Drunken Bricklayer" vase by Geoffrey Baxter, Whitefriars Glassworks, c.1966, ht 21cm/8¹/₄in, **£90–110/$135–165**

"Bark" vase by Geoffrey Baxter,
Whitefriars Glassworks, c.1966,
ht 15cm/6in, **£20–25/$30–40**

▲ "Bark" vase by Geoffrey Baxter

This design is from the first
series of textured mould-blown
glass by Geoffrey Baxter which
was produced from 1967. The
original idea for the piece
came to him on a walk in
the woods during which he
collected bark that he used
to make a mould. Baxter
was unsure of how his new
planned range would be
received by his superior at
Whitefriars, W. J. Wilson, so
he produced the prototypes
in a number of colours while
Wilson was away on holiday.
The designs were accepted
and became very successful,
injecting the company with
a new impetus.

▼ Vase by R. Stennet-Willson

This vase is part of a series of
textured wares originally
designed by Stennet-Willson
for his company, Kings Lynn
Glass. This piece, however,
bares the acid-etched mark
of Wedgwood Glass who
took over the company in
1969. Pieces from this
range are often mistaken
for Whitefriars glassware,
however, Stennet-Willson
does not, on the whole,
produce such deep relief
work as Baxter. This Kings
Lynn/Wedgwood ware has a
style all of its own, and is
notable for the controlled
restraint employed in the
apparently randomly arranged
panels of textured glass.

Vase by Ronald Stennet-Willson,
Wedgwood Glass, c.1969,
ht 21cm/8¹/₄in, **£38–48/$60–70**

Vase by Helena Tynell, Riihimäki,
c.1960, ht 17.5cm/6³/₄in,
£60–70/$90–105

▲ Vase by Helena Tynell

This flask-shaped vase, with its
sunburst design, is part of a
very successful series of
textured vases designed by
Helena Tynell (b.1918) in the
mid-to late-1960s. Some
reference material suggests
that it was designed as a juice
carafe, although its flat wide
rim appears to be entirely
unsuitable for pouring. This
piece has in the past been
mistakenly attributed to
Geoffrey Baxter, as it is very
like some of his pieces in
appearance, and has a similar
style pontil and rim finish.

▼ Vase by Constance Spry

Constance Spry (1886–1960), the doyenne of flower arranging in post-war Britain, was invited by Wedgwood and Stevens & Williams to design vases for flower arranging. Her pieces usually bare a facsimile signature along with the factory mark, unlike those of consultant designer and architect Keith Murray, whose pieces were often left unsigned. This was probably due to retailers who stipulated their requirements to the manufacturer, rather than an indication that the piece is a second.

Vase by Constance Spry, Royal Brierley (Stevens & Williams), c.1960, ht 13.5cm/5¹/₄in, **£40–50/$60–75**

Vase by Frank Thrower, Dartington Glass, c.1968, ht 11cm/4¹/₄in, **£20–30/$30–45**

▲ Vase by Frank Thrower

Frank Thrower (1932–87) was responsible for nearly all the Dartington glass designs produced during his twenty years at the company. This vase dates from between 1967, when the company began, to about 1970. Much Dartington glass of the period was clear, and had a Scandinavian influence as a result of Thrower's travels in Sweden and Finland in the 1960s. This hexagonal, "midnight"-coloured vase, with its stylized flower motif, is a good example of his simple and unpretentious style. Some of his stemware displays traits of another strong influence on his work; 18th century English glass.

FACT FILE

• Each time a wooden mould is used to produce a textured piece of glass, it will burn a little, so that the pieces produced first are more faithful to the original mould. Later pieces may have a less defined surface which can adversely affect its value.

▼ Vase by Jones & Co., Birmingham

This square vase, produced in Sweden for the import company Jones & Co of Birmingham, imitates and capitalizes on Geoffrey Baxter's popular designs for Whitefriars. Being self-coloured, it was cheap to produce and could be competitively priced in order to rival the Whitefriars ranges. However, it differs from these as it is not cased. Occasionally pieces are found with an original label bearing the company name.

Vase by Jones & Co., 1969, Birmingham, (manufactured in Sweden), ht 17cm/6³/₄in, **£18–24/ $30–40**

Mould-blown angular

Most angular mould-blown glass, with some notable earlier exceptions, was designed and produced during the late 1960s and 1970s, and while not a glass making technique as such, forms a stylistic body of work that conformed to a contemporary aesthetic loosely related to Pop Art. The form is seen in Scandinavian, Czech, Italian, and American glass, but is not readily discernible as a British trait. In addition to pieces from these countries, there are notable examples by Carlo Moretti in Italy and René Roubicek in Czechoslovakia (Czech Republic). The variations on what is essentially a cylindrical form are many, and the decorative effects used are equally varied. These pieces are often bought by collectors to enhance 1960s Pop Art style interiors, and are generally affordable.

Vase by Timo Sarpaneva, Iittala, c.1958, ht 25.5cm/10in, **£100–125/ $150–190**

▼ Vase by Timo Sarpaneva
This glass stems from the "i-glass" line of wares designed by Timo Sarpaneva (b.1926), beginning in 1956. The range displays a flare for form and functionality, making it both a design and commercial success. Colours included amethyst, blue, grey-green, lilac, and smoke, and customers were encouraged to choose a mixture of coloured glasses to produce harlequin sets. All the items in the series were thin-blown and involved moulds in the production process. In this carafe-like vase, the intensity of the colour alters with the varying thickness of the glass.

Vase by Blenko, c.1960s, ht 34cm/13¹/₄in, **£60–70/$90–$105**

▶ Vase by Blenko
This orange vase, with its fine random bubbling, illustrates Blenko's ability to reflect contemporary trends. Its bright colour and quirky form mirror the style of the Pop Art movement. It is noticeably higher than an average vase, allowing it to make more of a "statement", and is typical of decorative objects used in interior design during this period.

Vase by Reijmyre, c.1960s, ht 17.5cm/6³/₄in, **£40–50/$60–$75**

▲ Vase by Reijmyre
The similarity of this Swedish vase to the vases from Riihimäki of Finland, known as "Lasi" vases, is quite striking (see right). The moulded central section portrays an attention to detail by the designer that gives the piece character and style. It is a cased coloured vase with a heavy clear base that refracts the light and lifts the whole piece, giving it a sparkle that would be lacking were it purely self-coloured.

▼ Vases by Riihimäki Glassworks
These vases are sometimes erroneously called "Lasi" vases (lasi meaning "glass" in Finnish), and the term has also begun to be used colloquially to refer to a whole range of glassware by Riihimäki, making the name somewhat confusing (see p.26). The aim of the designers of these pieces was to produce wares that were aesthetically pleasing as well as useful and affordable. This shape is easily available today, an indication of its popularity at the time of its manufacture.

Vases by Riihimäki Glassworks, c.1960s, **£30–40/$45–60**

FACT FILE

- Most of the pieces shown here, and variations by other factories and designers, are readily available.
- First recognized for their value as interior design accessories, these pieces have only recently begun to be collected.

"Palette" vase by Per Lütken, Holmegaard, c.1969, ht 15.5cm/6in, **£40–50/$60–75**

▲ "Palette" vase by Per Lütken
The "Palette" series by Per Lütken (1916–98) were white with a transparent coloured casing, or opaque coloured glass, and came in a variety of shapes which became more complex the taller they grew. They were produced by Holmegaard in tandem with the "Carnaby" range, with which it has stylistic similarities.

Cut glass

The post-war era saw great divergence in cut glass, with distinct styles emerging from Britain, Scandinavia, and Czechoslovakia (Czech Republic). In Britain, designers were encouraged by the Harrods Exhibition of 1934 and the Festival of Britain in 1951 to continue to challenge the traditional Victorian approach to cutting. They introduced simplified designs that echoed contemporary art themes and accentuated the shapes of vessels. In Czechoslovakia, abstract designs were used to great effect, although Czech glass from this period is now scarce. Scandinavian countries approached cutting differently, taking care not to over cut in order to complement the shape of the vessel or utilize its reflective capabilities.

Vase by John Luxton, Stuart & Sons Ltd., c.1950, ht 17.5cm/6³/₄in, **£120–150/$180–225**

▶ **Vase by John Luxton**
This bold design by John Luxton (b.1920) uses a simple, curved barrel form decorated with polished roundels that alternate with simple, deep cut vertical lines. Luxton was responsible for most of Stuart's designs between 1949 and 1985, his styles changing markedly with each successive decade, reflecting the prevailing tastes of the times. However, throughout his time at Stuart's, he also continued designing for their traditional cut ranges.

▼ **Bowl by William Wilson & Bernard Fitch**
William Wilson (1914–72) collaborated with Bernard Fitch from the Whitefriars cutting workshop to produce this free-blown and cut bowl with bands of broad, oval and vertical mitre-cutting. This "monumental" style appealed to both traditional and contemporary tastes, although it eventually gave way to Geoffrey Baxter's lighter cutting style.

Bowl by William Wilson & Bernard Fitch, Whitefriars Glassworks, c.1950, dia. 22.5cm/8³/₄in, **£150–180/$225–270**

- Czech and Scandinavian cut glass of the post-war period currently has more international appeal and recognition than British cut glass, and despite its high quality, is overlooked and undervalued.

▼ Vase by Geoffrey Baxter

This vase was part of Whitefriars' response to the popular glassware emerging from the Stourbridge factories at this time. Geoffrey Baxter felt that it was necessary to add cut glass to Whitefriars' repertoire in order to be commercially competitive. While some of the designs that were produced were rather traditional, this vase is one of the pieces that have a restrained contemporary aesthetic. The discreet star cuts – a recurring 1950s motif – are a perfect foil for the simple, polished, mitre-cut diagonal lines.

Vase by Geoffrey Baxter, Whitefriars Glassworks, c.1956, ht 19.5cm/6³/₄in,
£100–125/$150–190

"Bodiam" vase by David Hammond, Thomas Webb, c.1970s, ht 17cm/6³/₄in.
£110–130/$165–195

▲ "Bodiam" vase by David Hammond

During his earlier work for Thomas Webb, David Hammond (b.1931) favoured a light approach, combining shallow intaglio cutting with engraving; and he worked closely with the blowers, cutters, and engravers in the company to produce his designs. When using cutting alone, his work could be quite bold, whether in the 1950s, or as here in this later piece from the 1970s. This heavy-based vase has been cut to accentuate the form using broad mitre-cutting in a simple grid, and alternating it with vertical decoration.

▼ Vase by Ingeborg Lundin

This piece by Ingeborg Lundin demonstrates her skilled use of line and form. The shape of the vase is asymmetrical and carefully considered. The simple line-cutting in a four way, criss-crossed, or "weaving", pattern, is placed on one face of the vessel alone, and only in one small off-centre patch. The result demonstrates considerable design awareness and sophistication.

Vase by Ingeborg Lundin, Orrefors, Sweden c.1959, ht 20cm/8in,
£80–100/$120–150

▼ Vase by Mona Morales-Schildt

This vase has been blown with a cased colour, and then optically cut into a flowing, sculptural form. The result is deceptively simple; this curved form is far more difficult to produce than a flat one. The convex, optical-cutting, combined with the internal colour, produces fascinating optical effects. Its style, more reminiscent of European glass than Scandinavian work of the time, is unsurprising, as Mona Morales-Schildt (1908–99) trained at the celebrated Venini factory in Italy (see p.22) in the 1950s, only joining Kosta in 1958.

Vase by Mona Morales-Schildt, Kosta, Sweden c.1960, ht 17cm/6³/₄in, **£320–380/ $480–570**

Vase by Tapio Wirkkala, Iittala, c.1955, ht 15cm/6in, **£150–180/$225–270**

▲ Vase by Tapio Wirkkala

This vase is part of a range designed by Tapio Wirkala (1915–85) inspired by the success of his limited edition series of "Kantarelli" vases for Iittala in 1946. The fine cut lines used to decorate these pieces, which echo the style of the earlier series, accentuate their sculptural nature and gentle curves to great effect. The original "Kantarelli" design has become a design icon, and these smaller, later pieces also have cachet, and are popular with collectors.

▼ Murano ashtray

The technique used to produce this ashtray was employed by the Czechs, the Italians, and the Swedes in various ranges made during this period. The first gather is the main colour (in this case red), which is then cased in a thin layer of another colour (here, amber), and finally heavily cased in clear glass. Items are then symmetrically facet-cut to a pre-determined shape. This heavily cased colour with a contrasting coloured "halo" is referred to as "sommerso". Considering the work involved, one might expect facet-cut sommerso pieces to be far more expensive than they are.

Murano ashtray, Italy c.1950s–'60s, l. 14cm/5¹/₂in, **£20–25/$30–40**

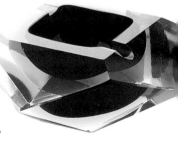

FACT FILE

• Typical post-war designs avoid traditional high-Victorian criss-cross cutting all over the item. Restrained or stylized designs with controlled cutting are important features to look for.

Vase by Irene Stevens, Webb Corbett, c.1950s, ht 15cm/6in, **£180–220/$270–330**

▲ Vase by Irene Stevens

The use of curving, diagonal mitre-cutting on what is almost a sphere exhibits the consummate skill of the cutter of this piece. The gently curving lines, echoed by a lighter intaglio-cut line, combine to form a rhythmic simplicity that conveys a feeling of movement. The cutting follows similar design ideals to those of the late-18th and early-19th centuries, in which simple cutting was used to accentuate the shape. The lightness of this design by Irene Stevens (b.1917) is aesthetically sophisticated and encapsulates the contemporary design approach that became synonymous with this company's production.

▼ Vase by Webb Corbett

At first sight this vase appears traditional with its realistic rendering of its subject matter, however, closer inspection reveals contemporary touches. The combination of mitre-cutting for the leaves and petals, with the unpolished intaglio work of the flower trumpets exhibits a strong understanding of the two techniques, and produces a style we now take for granted. The designer is unknown, but it is the outstanding quality of workmanship rather than the attribution that matters here.

Vase by Webb Corbett, c.1957, ht 23cm/9in, **£100–120/ $150–180**

"Random" vase by David Queensbury, Webb Corbett, c.1963, ht 6.5cm/2¹/₂in, **£35–42/$55–65**

▲ "Random" vase by David Queensbury

Webb Corbett commissioned David Queensbury (b.1929), Professor of Ceramics & Glass at the RCA in London, to design a range of cut glass that would extend, rather than break with tradition. "Random" pattern, one of the resulting designs, is made up of evenly spaced vertical cuts running from base to rim, with horizontal cuts at irregular intervals.

Engraved glass

The post-war era saw the continued use of engraved glass patterns from the inter-war years, as well as a new restrained abstract style. Favoured motifs of the past, such as figurative images, were still evident, but were now joined by images from the modern world, for example the skyscrapers of Manhattan used by Vicke Lindstrand. Much of the work available today is wheel-engraved, which can be produced in factories, as well as by individual designers. The less common diamond-point engraving is executed by hand, and so lends itself to individual work. Much engraved glass of this period was influenced by Scandinavian design, although some astonishing work originated in Czechoslovakia (Czech Republic) whose craftsmen produced modern designs inspired by their own world-renowned tradition.

▼ **Vase by Ernest Gordon**
Ernest Gordon (b.1926) worked for Åfors from the mid-1950s through to the early 1960s, and produced glassware using a variety of techniques. This piece reflects his restrained style and his understanding of prevailing Scandinavian organic design. The shape of the vase is fairly commonplace, but is given a lift by the asymmetric line and finely engraved groups of more or less vertical lines, which suggests the icy Swedish landscape.

Vase by Ernest Gordon,
Åfors, c.1955,
ht 18.5cm/7¹/₄in,
£180–220/$270–330

Vase by Sven Palmquist,
Orrefors, c.1960,
ht 22.5cm/8³/₄in,
£85–110/$130–165

▶ **Vase by Sven Palmquist**
The figure and bird on this vase by Sven Palmquist are juxtaposed in such a way that there appears to be space and height between them. This feeling of perspective is the result of the skills of both the engraver and the designer. The figures would have been drawn onto the glass, and the deepest areas engraved first, followed by the rest of the image. Muscular detail would then have been drawn and engraved, and lastly, the fine detail worked and polished.

• Much engraved glass can be identified by incised or acid-etched factory marks or signatures, or else by reference to catalogues. Occasionally glass-makers' labels will have survived.

Vase by John Selbing, Orrefors, c.1958, ht 24.5cm/9¹/₂in, **£100–120/$150–180**

Bowl by Ingeborg Lundin, Orrefors, c.1954, dia. 11cm/4¹/₂in, **£65–75/$100–115**

▲ **Bowl by Ingeborg Lundin**
The irregular, dented surface of this bowl by Ingeborg Lundin facilitates the design of random wheel-engraved roundels with dipped centres. A grinding wheel was run over a high spot to make an unpolished circular motif. This has the surreal effect of making the viewer unsure whether the centre is actually dipped or protruding, depending on the angle of view. This contortion evokes the memory of the molten malleability of glass, and is typical of Lundin's exploration of abstract engraving combined with form.

▼ **Bowl by Strömbergshyttan**
The fish motif was a favourite subject of engravers during the 20th century, probably because glass, with its clarity and plasticity, is an excellent medium for suggesting watery seascapes. Usually clear or very pale blue glass is used, but here a transparent dark amber (or brown) colour has been employed to portray a riverbed. The water weeds are wheel-engraved and polished, while the fish have been left unpolished, with polished detail.

Bowl by Strömbergshyttan, c.1950s, dia. 21.5cm/8¹/₂in, **£80–100/$120–150**

▶ **Vase by John Selbing**
The elongated motif of sails and rigging echoes the typically attenuated shape of this vase by John Selbing (b.1908). The interplay of the solid sails with the lined rigging has his characteristic lightness of touch. Selbing's understanding of glass stems from his time as the photographer of Orrefors products, during which he became famous for his ability to capture the qualities of glass on film. This affinity for glass was enhanced by a close working relationship with the Orrefors craftsmen.

Bowl by Täpio Wirkkala, Iittala, c.1950s, ht 5.5cm/2¹/₄in, **£120–150/$180–225**

▲ Bowl by Täpio Wirkkala
The subtle diffused look of this bowl is achieved by using a copper wheel to cut shallow, unpolished diagonal lines over the outer surface. The resulting effect softens the severe external form, which is contrasted against the curved internal surface to give the bowl a sculptural integrity. The shiny inner surface and rim allow the light to refract through the glass, and the engraved outer surface diffuses it. In this bowl Täpio Wirkkala has used a simple form to great effect, and it is the understanding of glass – its technical and aesthetic possibilities – that makes him one of the most collectable designers of this era.

▼ Vase by Geoffrey Baxter
This vase is one of several fish designs by Geoffrey Baxter that are often mistaken for Scandinavian work. The fish moving through weed is suggested by sparse, fine, wheel-engraved curved lines, each fish represented by a single unpolished sweep of the wheel, the fins and mouths added afterwards.
It is a simple and yet effective design, and economic to produce. These pieces are now often overlooked in favour of Baxter's coloured wares.

Vase by Geoffrey Baxter, Whitefriars Glassworks, c.1956, ht 26cm/10¹/₄in, **£80–120/ $120–180**

Vase by Vicke Lindstrand, Kosta, c.1955, ht 18cm/7in, **£100–120/$150–180**

▲ Vase by Vicke Lindstrand
The curvilinear organic form of this vase by Vicke Lindstrand (1904–83) is typical of Swedish glass of this period. The fine linear pattern, with its delicate seed heads scattered across the surface of the vase, captures and refracts light, giving another dimension to the form. The design and engraving have a lightness of touch that suggests grass waving in the wind, a motion exaggerated by the pattern on one side being visible through the other.

FACT FILE

- Scratches or digs will interfere with the image and cannot be removed, and these, together with discolouration from use, will affect the value of an engraved item. Cracks may well be disguised by the engraving, so check items carefully before purchase.

▼ Brandy glass by Peter Dreiser

Between 1955 and 1970 Peter Dreiser (b.1936) produced a series of numbered identical patterns engraved on glasses (often supplied by Whitefriars) as limited editions. Unlike conventional engraved pictures produced from a plate made by the artist, each pattern was engraved separately. Subjects included animals, birds, fish, and flowers. In 1970 Dreiser set up his own specialist workshop and now produces prized, specially commissioned pieces. These glasses present an opportunity for collectors to have an example of his work at a reasonable price.

Brandy glass by Peter Dreiser, c.1962, ht 14cm/5¹/₂in, **£70–85/$105–$130**

Vase by Vicke Lindstrand, Kosta, c.1955, ht 27cm/10¹/₂in, **£240–300/$360–450**

▲ Vase by Vicke Lindstrand

Vicke Lindstrand's technique of using both sides of a vase to produce a single image that could be viewed from a particular vantage point is employed to great effect in this vase. The bulk of the image is roughed out by acid-etching, prior to more detail being added using wheel engraving, and then left unpolished. Polished detail is then added, but only on one side of the vase. This device gives the illusion of perspective, as the closest point of the image has the sharpest detail.

▼ Commemorative goblet by W. J. Wilson

W. J. Wilson is credited with re-introducing diamond-point engraving to Whitefriars in the 1930s. He engraved all the commemorative editions of goblets he was involved in while at the company, including this one for the 1953 coronation of Queen Elizabeth II, which features his distinctive style of outlined, cross-hatched lettering. Many collectors of art glass do not subscribe to commemorative wares, although good quality pieces of this kind are prized by those who do.

Commemorative goblet by W.J. Wilson, Whitefriars Glassworks, c.1953, ht 20.5cm/8in, **£65–85/ $100–$130**

Tableware

Tableware from the 17th and 18th centuries has been a traditional area of glass collecting, with glasses and decanters being particularly popular items. Collecting from the post-war period often concentrates on vases and bowls, which consequently pushes up prices, leaving tableware as a viable alternative for new collectors. Decanters, candlesticks, water jugs, and even single glasses can be put together to form a collection that reflects a good cross-section of the styles of the period. Or you might choose to focus on the work of a single country, factory, or series. If you wish to build up a complete service for use, be aware that some patterns are scarcer than others; a reputable dealer can advise and perhaps help form your collection.

Carafe by Vicke Lindstrand, Kosta, c.1955, ht 29cm/11¹/₂in, **£70–90/$120–$140**

▶ **Carafe by Vicke Lindstrand**
The adaptation of a flattened ovoid form exploits a popular Scandinavian shape to produce a simple, effective design. The vessel is formed by cutting the opening on a slant, and polishing the rim, with the addition of another piece of glass to produce the spout. This piece by Vicke Lindstrand typifies the influential Modern Scandinavian style, with its cohesive blend of simple strong form and ergonomic functionality.

▼ **Decanter by Tapio Wirkkala**
The formal geometric shape of this decanter by Tapio Wirkkala is complemented by its stark spherical brass stopper, made from a solid ball of metal over a disc onto which a cork "peg" is screwed. The heavy brass, an unusual choice in this context, combines with the deep amethyst glass base to produce a strong and unusual design.

Decanter by Tapio Wirkkala, Iittala, c.1958, ht 23cm/9in, **£120–140/$180–210**

FACT FILE

- Jugs are readily available and often affordable due to their utilitarian nature. Look out for cracks in the body and chipped spouts.
- Check whether or not an ice bucket would have originally had a metal liner. Many from this period do not, but a missing liner will devalue the item.

▼ "Ultima Thule" carafe & glasses by Tapio Wirkkala

This range was originally designed by Wirkkala for the airline Finnair to commemorate transatlantic flights, and was exclusive to the airline in 1967. It was put into commercial production the following year, and the carafe was introduced in 1970. The form of the carafe resembles Wirkkala's decanter on the previous page, however, its wider neck and textured surface, which incorporate little feet, transform it. Both examples reflect Wirkkala's background as a sculptor and together represent his versatility as a designer.

Carafe & glasses by Tapio Wirkkala, Iittala, c.1964, ht 15cm/6in, **£85–95/$130–145**

"Assimetrico" glass by Joe Colombo, c.1965, **£25–35/$35–50**

▲ "Assimetrico" glass by Joe Colombo

The design concept behind this glass is now rather dated. Italian designer Joe Colombo (1930–71) designed the glass to allow the user to hold it and a cigarette using only one hand, simply by positioning the stem off-centre and to the edge of the glass's diameter. The thickened stem and cantilevered bowl produce a fluid sculptural form that remains very distinctive, and is just as modern in appearance as it was when first produced.

▼ Ice bucket by Gerda Strömberg

This ice bucket is typical of Gerda Strömberg's (1879–1960) controlled designs with cut and polished rims. Like many of her deceptively simple designs, the geometric form is softened by curves. The thick walls and the pale silvery-blue colour seen in this piece are a notable feature of her work for the company.

Ice bucket by Gerda Strömberg, Strömbergshyttan, c.1960, dia. 15cm/6in, **£60–80/$90–120**

▼ Decanter & glasses by Ronald Stennet-Willson

The design of this decanter has been thoroughly considered. Its efficient stopper, with its smooth, tapered shape, fits any decanter in this range, making for economy of manufacture. Its dimpled surface allows the item to be gripped easily – an approach that was used successfully by Arts and Crafts designers around 1900. Despite being a British designer, Stennet-Willson has produced a design with a wholly Modern Scandinavian approach for this-London based import company.

Decanter & glasses by Ronald Stennet-Willson, Wuidart, c.1950s, ht 17cm/6³/₄in (decanter) ht 5cm/2in (glasses), **£48–60/ $75–90**

Decanter by Kjell Blomberg, Gullaskruf Glassworks, c.1954, ht 24.5cm/9¹/₂in, **£120–140/$180–210**

▲ Decanter by Kjell Blomberg

This mould-blown decanter by Kjell Blomberg (b.1931) was produced by Gullaskruf who supplied it to the glass importers Wuidart. Both the decanter's shape and the raised drinking glass motif were made by blowing glass into a mould. Its brass stopper and cork peg follow a traditional style, but have been adapted to match the 1950s design.

▼ Decanter by Erik Höglund

Many of the best Scandinavian glass designers were also artists, or sculptors like Erik Höglund (1932–2001), who had an innate feel for the sculptural quality of glass. Höglund is rather underrated today, as his work can be seen as being somewhat heavy in approach. During the post-war period, however, his revolutionary primitive style shocked the world of glass design. His appointment at Boda in 1953 revitalized the company. Embracing modern art, Höglund often repeated and played with the motifs and stylistic features of his work.

Decanter by Erik Höglund, Boda Glassworks, (Kosta), c.1965, ht 27cm/10¹/₂in, **£150–180/$225–270**

• While chipped
stoppers devalue a
decanter, missing or
replacement stoppers
reduce the value
significantly. Stoppers
must both match the
base and fit snugly.
• Stained insides can
rarely be cleaned by
ordinary methods.
Check that a decanter is
clear by holding it up to
the light.

Decanter & glasses by Podebrady
Glassworks, c.1950s,
ht 27cm/10¹/₂in (decanter),
ht 6cm/2¹/₄in,
£150–180/$225–270

▲ Decanter & glasses by Podebrady Glassworks

This polished decanter with
matching schnapps or liqueur
glasses reflects the style and
quality of cut glass that was
being produced in
Czechoslovakia (now the Czech
Republic) during the 1950s.
The decanter has a
contemporary shape,
and the stopper is
typical of Czech
design from the
period. The fact that this
set is not attributed to a
designer does not detract
from its quality or
intrinsic value.

▼ Decanter & glasses by Bengt Orup

The use of heavily ribbed,
wrythen, (or twisted), stems
to glasses, decanter bases and
stoppers, carafes and water
jugs was very fashionable in
clear glassware in the late
1950s. Here Bengt Orup
(b.1916) has echoed the
shape of the twisted (or flame)
stopper in the stems of the
glasses. Both are formed from
a twisted, flattened piece of
glass, giving the set a unity
of design.

Decanter & glasses by Bengt Orup,
Johansfors, c.1950s,
ht 27.5cm/10³/₄in (decanter),
ht 15cm/6in (glasses),
£120–140/$180–210

"Aristocrat" decanter
& "Canada" glass
by Per Lütken,
Holmegaard, c.1958,
ht 37.5cm/14³/₄in
(decanter),
ht 13cm/5in (glasses),
**£125–150/
$190–225**

▶ Decanter & glass by Per Lütken

This stretched-form
decanter, in one
of the favoured
colours from
the Holmegaard
palette, became
very popular,
and is still much
sought after today by 1950s
and 60s enthusiasts. Per
Lütken's designs for the
flattened stopper and the body
of the decanter are both
ergonomic and at the same
time deeply sculptural.
The stopper, with its pierced,
offset hole, shows particular
reference to contemporary
art of the period.

Candleholder by Geoffrey Baxter, Whitefriars Glassworks, c.1965, ht 23.5cm/9¹/₄in, **£24–32/$36–48**

▲ **Candleholder by Geoffrey Baxter**
This two-piece candleholder, with its base and separate tapering chimney, capitalized on the fashion for using candles as table centres. First mention of this piece is made in the 1966 catalogue where midnight blue (shown) and shadow green were introduced. Pewter and ruby followed, and later lilac. These appear to be an addition to the company's thin-blown wares, designed mainly by Baxter, from 1961–63.

▼ **Candelabra by Michel Daum**
The "flying bar" shape of this candelabra by Michel Daum (b.1910) is so susceptible to breakage, it is rather surprising that this one has survived. In this example, to prevent cracks and reduce wax retention, a metal disc has been placed in the bottom of each holder. This piece was produced by a combination of hot-blowing and mould-blowing, and was cut and polished to finish.

Candelabra by Michel Daum, Cristallerie Daum, c.1950s, l. 29cm/11¹/₂in, **£150–180/$225–270**

Candlesticks by Ronald Stennet-Willson, Kings Lynn, 1967–68 and Wedgwood, 1969, ht (left to right) 14.5cm/5³/₄in, 21cm/8¹/₄in, 10.5cm/4in, **£20–48/$30–75**

▲ **Candlesticks by Ronald Stennet-Willson**
These candlesticks were designed by Stennet-Willson for Kings Lynn Glass prior to its takeover by Wedgwood. The "Brancaster" (left) has a hollow stem and comes in three sizes. The squat, hollow-knopped amber holder (right) was produced in only one size. The multi-disc "Sheringham" (centre) came in various sizes, and was particularly difficult to make. It received considerable critical acclaim and public attention when it was first produced.

- Beware of damage to sconces and holders produced by burning candles. Check for cracks by holding the item up to the light. Note that damage can sometimes be hidden by old wax.
- Historically, holders sold as pairs tend to be regarded as being more valuable, however, this is of less significance with post-war pieces

▼ Candlestick by Kjell Blomberg

During the late 1960s there was a fashion for textured glass, most of which came from Finland. However, designers from other countries were also experimenting with surface decoration. Kjell Blomberg (b.1931), who worked at Gullaskruf in Sweden, was one such exponent. The candlestick seen here was made by blowing coloured glass into a mould, resulting in a hollow tree-like form. The base has a ground edge and incised foot, and designer marks on the underside.

Candlestick by Kjell Blomberg, Gullaskruf, c.1960s, ht 17.5cm/6³/₄in, **£30–40/$45–60**

Candleholder by Bertil Vallien, Åfors, c.1960s, dia. 11cm/4¹/₄in, **£40–50/$60–75**

▲ Candleholder by Bertil Vallien

In 1963 Bertil Vallien (b.1938) joined Afors, which merged with Kosta in 1964 and Boda in 1971, and eventually became known as Åforsgruppen AB. Vallien himself went on to become one of the most important and formative designers in the Swedish glass industry. This clear candleholder is one of his earlier pieces for the company and is hot-blown into a mould. The circle of decoration on its shaped underside is made of raised nodules, while its smooth upper surface falls towards a central hole in which the candle sits. The shape of the holder and its decoration reflect and refract light shed from the candle.

▼ "Festivo" candlesticks by Timo Sarpaneva

This successful design by Timo Sarpaneva was produced for over two decades, and is typical of the late 1960s vogue for textured surface glass. Its surface was the product of a charred wood mould, and resembles either wood or bark, or perhaps frosted ice. Available in various sizes, its wide flattened conical base is echoed by the slightly narrower top.

"Festivo" candlesticks by Timo Sarpaneva, Iittala, c.1964, ht 18.5cm/7¹/₄in, **£38–48/$60–75**

Manufactured glass

Machine-made glass may lack the spontaneity and individuality of hand-blown wares, but much of it was not only well made, but also the result of ground-breaking manufacturing techniques. Our familiarity with many of these products often blinds us to the innovative nature of some of the series, such as Orrefors "Fuga" ware and Chance Bros. "Fiesta" glass, at the time of their production. The types of products available are also quite varied, ranging from press-moulded pieces through to centrifugally formed items and screen-printed wares; and although initially mass-produced, items from some ranges are now quite rare. For the collector, machine-made glass can offer affordable style.

Vase by Lars Hellsten. Skrufs, c.1960s, ht 20.5cm/8in, **£40–50/ $60–75**

◀ **Vase by Lars Hellsten**
Lars Hellsten (b.1933) became one of the leading exponents of the "neo-baroque" or "pop-baroque" glass style of which this vase is an example. Originally a ceramicist and sculptor, Hellsten worked for the Swedish company Skrufs between 1964 and 1972. His background as a sculptor lent itself to this form of work, since before an iron or aluminium mould could be made, a model had to be produced in plaster or clay.
The scrolling design for this vase, contrasting flattened areas with pitted patterning, is typical of Hellsten's work for Skrufs.

Celery vase by Jack L. Barnett Ltd., England c.1951, ht 18cm/7in, **£18–24/$27–36**

▶ **Celery vase by Jack L. Barnett Ltd.**
This press-moulded vase was part of the "Barnock" range produced to commemorate the 1951 Festival of Britain. The rather unexceptional vase is made collectable because of Abram Games' well-known symbol for the exhibition. Although thousands of these vases were made, few remain, making them sought after, particularly by collectors of Festival ephemera. The word "celery" was embossed near the rim of the vase, allowing it to be classified as utilitarian ware, thus avoiding restrictions on "luxury" glass imposed after World War II.

• Machine made glass is generally overlooked, despite creating an opportunity to form an affordable and stylish collection.

• Look for items that use forms and styles that are readily identifiable as of the period, but beware of modern "retro" pieces.

Press-moulded vases, Czechoslovakia, c.1962, ht 18.5cm/7¹/₄in, **£18–25/$30–40** (left), c.1970, ht 14cm/5¹/₂in, **£20–30/$30–45**, (right)

▲ Press-moulded vases, Czechoslovakia (Czech Republic)

These press-moulded vases, produced in the 1960s and 1970s, are representative of Czechoslovakia (Czech Republic) glass from the mid-1950s. The abstract patterns resemble cut glass from the period, but these mass-produced, manufactured items were both plentiful and affordable, and, until recently, largely disregarded by collectors. The piece on the left was deisgned by Frantisek Vízner (b.1936), and that on the right by Jiri Repásek (b.1927). Its fluid interlocking pattern is typical of Repásek's deep relief abstract work from 1965 to 1985.

▼ "Fuga" bowl by Sven Palmquist

The austere sculptural lines of this "Fuga" piece by Sven Palmquist are typical of 1950s Scandinavian style. The idea for his design dates back to 1934, however, because of resistance within Orrefors to machine-made products, the series was not produced until 1954, and then to international acclaim. The glass is spun centrifugally, so that it is forced up the sides of the mould evenly, resulting in consistent quality and thickness. The range of simple, stylish bowls, vases, and tableware was produced in transparent or opaque glass, and some ranges within the series include both types.

"Fuga" bowl by Sven Palmquist, Orrefors, c.1954, dia. 16cm/6¹/₄in, **£25–35/$40–55**

Conical glasses by Alexander Hardie-Williamson, Allied Glass, c.1956–74, ht 11.5cm/4¹/₂in, **£3–5/$5–8**

▲ Conical glasses by Alexander Hardie-Williamson

Hardie-Williamson (1907–94) was an industrial designer who reflected the prevailing designs of the period. His work was not widely recognized until the 1996 exhibition of his work at Broadfield House Glass Museum in the UK, and his inclusion in the "Austerity to Affluence" show at the Fine Arts Society/Target Gallery. Despite this, his glasses still tend to be overlooked by collectors.

▼ "Slim Jims" by Alexander Hardie-Williamson

The work of Alexander Hardie-Willamson provides the opportunity to form a collection that represents glass design throughout the 1950s and 1960s. He produced 1,711 designs for Sherdley and Ravenshead alone between 1944 and 1974, some of which are still in production. Tumblers from Allied Glass also bear Hardie-Williamson's distinctive screen-prints, including "Slim Jims" (shown here), "Conicals" (or "Coolers"), "Chubbies", and "Chunkies".

"Slim Jims" by Alexander Hardie-Williamson, Allied Glass, c.1956–74, ht 14cm/5¹/₂in, **£4–8/$6–12 each**

Tricorn bowl by Nazeing, c.1970, l. 17cm/6¹/₄in, **£6–12/$10–18**

▲ Tricorn bowl by Nazeing

This press-moulded bowl came in various colours, with a separate, clear glass flower guide, and was probably produced for Boots the Chemist in the UK. It may derive from moulds that came into Nazeing's possession when they bought Sowerby's in 1972, which would mean that the design has its roots in the 1960s. Nazeing also owned half of Davidson's in the early 1950s, so the mould and design may be earlier still. Both these companies had produced similar bowls, but the shape of this one is more consistent with 1950s design.

▼ "Randi" bowl & vase by Arthur Percy

This press-moulded glassware by Arthur Percy (1886–1976) was consistent with Gullaskruf's tradition of producing well-designed pressed glass. In the "Randi" range, Percy translated the fluid lines from this period into mass-produced, everyday household items; his restrained use of alternating groups of linear patterning enhancing the line of the item. It was produced in transparent and opaque versions, and both remain affordable for today's collector.

"Randi" vase & bowl by Arthur Percy, Gullaskruf, c.1950s, ht 13cm/5in (left) ht 16cm/6¹/₄in (right), **£30–40/$45–60 each**

"Fiesta" giraffe carafe & lidded box by Chance Bros., c.1955, ht 30.5cm/12in (carafe), dia. 13.5cm/5$1/_4$in (box),
£20–30/ $30–45

▲ **"Fiesta" giraffe carafe & lidded box by Chance Bros.**
The "Fiesta" range was produced as an alternative to traditional press-moulded glassware. Its contemporary style, with its modern screen-printed designs, became very popular after its introduction at the 1951 Ideal Home Exhibition in London. It was cheaply mass-produced from 24oz. sheet glass, which was cut into shape and decorated by screen-printing, before being shaped in the kiln by "sag-bending". "Swirl" was the first truly contemporary pattern made by Chance as a full tableware set in 1955. Other patterns included "Night Sky" by Margaret Casson (b.1913).

▼ **"Smiley" & psychedelic screen printed tumblers**
Among the prevailing design themes of the 1960s were the acid colours and swirling patterns of psychedelia, seen here decorating the tumblers below. The "Smiley" pattern was designed by Harvey Ball (1922–2001), an American graphic artist who was commissioned by an American insurance company in 1963 to produce badges for its employees as a corporate image and morale booster. This simple design with a message was extremely successful – appearing on t-shirts, stickers, glassware, and many other products. The psychedelic and the "Smiley" designs represent some of the most iconic symbols of the 1960s.

FACT FILE

• Manufactured glass was produced in vast quantities, so be very particular about damage. Screen printed designs and gilded edges (such as Fiesta ware) should not be worn, scratched, or rubbed.
• Liquids should not be left in the vessel for longer than necessary, and avoid using dishwashers.

"Smiley" & psychedelic screen printed tumblers, 1960s,
£3–5/$5–8 each

Figurative glass

Animals, birds, and the human figure were favourite subjects for 20th century glass-makers. Post-war glass-making was particularly figurative because of the trend for designers to explore the sculptural possibilities of glass. Italian companies, such as Barovier, Segoso, and Venini, were masters at producing designer figurative pieces, which were often imitated by companies catering for the souvenir market. These souvenirs tended to be more flamboyant than the designer wares, and embraced a much wider spectrum of colours. The Scandinavians, on the other hand, were typically restrained in their use of colour, and employed a rather quirky approach to their designs, often producing figure-shaped, but functional vessels. British figurative glass from this period tends to be on the fringe of novelty glass, or have a bias toward paperweight forms.

"People" decanter by Erik Höglund, Boda Glassworks, 1956, ht 25cm/9³/₄in, **£40–50/$60–75**

► **"People" decanter by Erik Höglund**
This decanter makes a good vehicle for a highly simplified figure. By adding shallow contoured arms to the body of the vessel, and an embossed stylized head from the stopper, Erik Höglund (1932–2001) uses this bottle-shaped decanter (sometimes called a "People bottle") to suggest a human figure. This quirky piece, typical of Scandinavian figurative work, was produced in both male and female versions, and in different sizes and colours, including green and clear.

▼ **Murano female figure**
Figures of this kind were produced for the souvenir market from the 1950s onwards, usually in male and female pairs. They are more valuable to today's collector if the pair is still intact, and earlier pieces, which tend to be more detailed and better quality, are more sought after. Each is made up of a number of pieces fused together while hot by a "chair" of workers. Complex pieces such as these are vulnerable, so look out for sharp edges and sections that may have been glued back on.

Murano female figure, 1950s–'60s, **£60–80/$90–120**

▼ **Vase by Holmegaard**

The form of this vase suggests a
highly simplified human figure.
The engraved facial features
and the leaf motif are both
typically Scandinavian. It is a
witty and stylish design,
following in the tradition of
Jacob Bang (1899–1965),
whose engraved work for
Holmegaard from between the
wars is very popular today. This
piece is by Ole Winther about
whom little is known. Whilst
following in Bang's tradition,
he also demonstrates an
awareness of Danish ceramic
designer Bjorn Winbald with
the stylistic features he uses

Vase by Holmegaard, c.1958,
ht 23cm/9in,
£80–120/$120–180

Female figure by Cedenese
Glass, c.1950s, ht 23cm/9in,
£240–300/$360–450

▲ **Female figure by
Cedenese Glass**

This female figure is part of an
enchanting group of stylized
peasants, made up of two
women and two men, which
represents the "Four Seasons".
All are made of clear glass with
a pink underlay, with some
areas picked out in gold foil. A
version with an emerald green
underlay is also known. They
are unsigned, but this figure
has a label for Cedenese
Glassworks, an Italian company.
These pieces are far more
sculptural and stylized than
their souvenir imitators.

• The varying
thicknesses of glass in
figurative pieces make
them vulnerable to water
temperatures. Clean with
a soft, soapy damp cloth
and a toothbrush for
crevices, rinse in tepid
water and dry on a
draining board.
• Pieces with an
individual or unusual
style are better buys than
mass-produced souvenirs.

▼ **Murano bird figure**

This stylized bird, the glass
simply pulled out to form its
features, is typical of Italian
figurative work of the 1950s
and 60s. It displays an
economy of form and
simplicity that distinguishes it
from many of the other more
complex figures produced for
the souvenir market.

Murano bird figure, Italy,
c.1950s–60s, ht 35cm/13³/₄in,
£40–50/$60–75

Miscellaneous glass

Utilitarian and novelty glass are usually thought to be unworthy of the serious collector, however, both have a collecting niche. Indeed kitsch novelty glass has a surprisingly large following, and post-war novelty glass prices have proved worth the investment on many occasions in recent years. Even those items which were originally designed for utilitarian rather than decorative purposes occasionally fetch good sale prices. At the time of their manufacture, many of the novelty items produced a steady, if modest income, for companies such as Vasart, and many firms, including Whitefriars Glassworks, found utilitarian objects such as lamp bases of equal commercial value.

Lamp base by Geoffrey Baxter, Whitefriars Glassworks, c.1960, ht 15.5cm/6in, **£65–75/ $100–115**

▼ **Lamp base by Geoffrey Baxter**
This lamp base is an adaptation of a vase by Geoffrey Baxter. Whitefriars created lamps throughout the 1930s, and many of their pieces could be used either as a lamp base or a vase. Earlier pieces incorporated a cork bung in the neck covered by a metal or wooden plate incorporating a bulb holder. This dual-use tradition was continued after the war with designs such as this one, a streaky "knobberly" version (see p.12), and a "Hoop" vase from the textured series. The latter two were made specifically as lamp bases, and therefore differed from the vases from the same series.

Lamp base, Italy, c.1950s, ht 58cm/22³/₄in, **£250–300/$375–450**

▶ **Lamp base, Italy**
This lamp base has a traditional look, and yet when it was produced it was quite innovative. The combination of deep ribbing with gold decoration and trapped bubbles is particularly effective. The technique, introduced by Ercole Barovier in the 1950s is known as the "Coro d'orta", and was also used for vases and bowls. Occasionally a coloured underlay was added, often in red, to dramatic effect. Not all pieces in this style are by Barovier since it was a successful and popular design, much copied by other factories.

Murano figurine, 1950s–'60s, ht 26cm/10¹/₄in, **£60–70/$90–105**

▲ Murano figurine
This colourful dog is typical of the novelty or souvenir wares produced on the island of Murano, near Venice, during the whole of the post-war era, right into the 1990s. Although produced at speed, many of these products exhibit the great skill of the workers who made them. Some pieces naturally lost quality in the rush to produce large numbers economically, but many, like this dog, have become collectors' items. Other subjects include clowns (inspired by Venini's *Commedia dell'arte* characters), cockerels, figures, and fish. The value of a piece will largely depend on the quality of the workmanship, and any damage will dramatically decrease it.

▼ Whisky bottle & basket by Vasart
Both these pieces are from the novelty ranges produced by Vasart Glass. The basket was one of the many affordable small dish designs which became the "bread and butter" earners for the firm. The whisky bottle was part of a range of advertising wares by Vasart, who, like Bell's Whisky, were located in Perth. It is probably an example of Bell's historical tradition of special Christmas packaging.

Bottle & basket by Vasart, c.1950s, ht 17cm/6³/₄in, **£30–40/ $45–60** (bottle), ht 9cm/3¹/₂in, **£20–30/ $30–45** (basket)

FACT FILE

- Legally, lamps should not be sold wired up unless by a qualified electrician, despite the fact that many collectors prefer original wiring. Always have the wiring checked before use.
- Check for sharp shiny edges on novelty glass, as damage to protruding surfaces disfigures and devalues an item and cannot be repaired.

"Loop" lamp base by Michel Daum, c.1950s, ht 42cm/16¹/₂in, **£140–160/$210–240**

▶ "Loop" lamp base by Michel Daum
This clear crystal, loop-shaped lamp base is anchored firmly in the Daum company's production of the period. Its clear sculptural form is typical of this factory's style and Michel Daum's (b.1910) designs in the post-war era, and is a complete departure from the firm's earlier work encompassing colour and techniques such as cameo and acid etching. The new style relied heavily on the clarity of the glass and its pliability, often incorporating, as seen here, a hot-formed plinth.

Designers, glass-makers, & marks

Much glass made during the 1940s, '50s and '60s is marked. However, some marks can be problematic, either because they are indistinct and difficult to identify, or because they were in the form of a paper label (usually missing). Check the base first, as the mark is often in the centre of the bottom of the piece or on the outside of the foot. If the mark is not obvious, hold the piece up to the light and turn it in various directions; a soft acid signature often shows up when the glass is held up against a piece of black cloth or card. Unmarked pieces have to be identified from company archives.

GREAT BRITAIN

Caithness Glass
1960s: labels with CG logo as shown.

Chance
Post-war labels printed Chance, Chance Glass, or Fiesta.

Dartington
Unmarked apart from Barware range, which is impressed on side of foot with D inside a square.
1960-80s logo: DG monogram and/or DARTINGTON ENGLAND

John Moncrieff Ltd (Monart)
(est. Perth, Scotland, 1865).
Monart Glass was unmarked except for pieces made for the American market, which occasionally have an acid-etched mark. Paper labels were used from 1930 to 1961 such as the one shown below.

Kings Lynn
Kings Lynn Glass unmarked until 1969 when a crown above the word Lynn was etched on foot and printed on labels.

LYNN

James Powell & Sons Ltd.
(est. London, 1834; from 1962 Whitefriars Glassworks; closed 1980). No marks or signatures; very occasionally original paper labels; identify items from archives.

Nazeing Glass
(est. London, 1928).
Identified by labels as shown.

Stevens & Williams
(est. Stourbridge, 1847; from 1930s known as "Royal Brierley").
Wares by Spry for the firm marked from 1960.

Strathearn
Marked with an impressed prunt showing a leaping salmon.

Stuart & Sons Ltd.
(est. Stourbridge, 1881).
Wares marked as shown from c.1926 to 1950.

ENGLAND

Mark below used from c.1930 to 1950.

ENGLAND

Thomas Webb & Sons
(est. Stourbridge, 1859).
Mark below used c.1935 to 1949.

Webb Corbett Ltd
(est. Stourbridge, 1897 as Thomas Webb & Corbett Ltd; from 1930s Webb Corbett Ltd).
Marks shown c.1930 to 1947(left), and 1947 to1965 (right).

Vasart
Vasart Glass c.1947–52: acid-etched Vasart in script. Vasart labels c.1952–56: printed Vasart. c.1956–64 shown below.

Wedgwood
Wedgwood Glass 1969-87 etched with Wedgwood, sometimes with the addition of England. Also various other labels.

Wedgwood Glass

Whitefriars Glass
Label c.1940–63 arched rectangle containing a friar with WHITEFRIARS above and CRYSTAL below. Label c.1950–63 as shown (left), and label 1963–80 (right):

CONTINENTAL EUROPE

Åfors

Post-war production pieces normally engraved with company name (Åfors until 1976, Kosta Boda since 1976), designer's name or monogram, pattern number, and sometimes date and edition.

Boda

Unmarked until 1953. Erik Höglund's designs are usually engraved H with a pattern number.

Cedenese

Usually unmarked but some pieces diamond engraved with designers surname or a fuller inscription, eg. Cedenese Antonio Da Ros 1960.

Daum

1960 onwards, incised: Daum France.

Ekenås

1940–47: modified circular label printed Ollers/EKENÅS/SWEDEN

Flygfors

Post-war art glass engraved Flygfors as shown. Usually with last two digits of year of production, and either range name or designer's surname. Kedelv indicates designs by Paul Kedelv made between 1949 and 1956. Coquille indicates designs made by Kedelv after 1956.

Hadeland

Post-war art glass normally engraved Hadeland with designer's initials, pattern number, or date. Logo and label as shown.

Holmegaard

Designs by Per Lütken engraved HG or Holmegaard, with either the

date of the design combined with the Lütken PL monogram (eg.19PL55), or a five digit pattern number by which pieces can be dated.

Johansfors

Usually unmarked but some art glass was engraved Johansfors with the pattern number and the designers surname.

Kosta

(est. Småland, Sweden, 1742). Engraved "Kosta" on base, designers name, or more usually monogram, and model number are also included.

Leerdam

(est. Leerdam, near Rotterdam, 1765; still operating). Pieces are usually signed with incised or acid-etched marks.

Mdina

1969–72 usually unmarked although some pieces carry an impressed Maltese Cross prunt.

Nuutajärvi

1946–53: art glass marked using an etching pen. 1954–65: art glass engraved. 1965–67: art glass unmarked. 1968 onwards: art glass engraved.

Orrefors

(est. Orrefors, Sweden, 1898) Engraved signature Orrefors; includes initials of the designer, along with date and series codes (numerical). Various labels.

Pukeberg

Until 1945: normally unmarked. Post-war art glass sometimes engraved with designer's name and year. Labels printed with Pukeberg logo and sometimes PUKEBERG/SWEDEN

Riihimäki

Logo from 1930s–60s lynx above RIIHIMÄKI logo.

Strömbergshyttan

Engraved S. hyttan, S-hyttan, Strömberg or Strömbershyttan, plus pattern number (composed of a letter indicating type of vessel), and a serial number which can be used to date designs.

Venini

1930 onwards: usually etched Venini/italia; venini/murano; venini/murano/MADE IN ITALY; or venini/murano/ars. Mid 1960s onwards: engraved or etched venini.

UNITED STATES

Blenko

Unmarked apart from sandblasted Blenko c.1959–60 and Designer's Studio Range engraved DS (for Don Shepherd) plus last two digits of year of production, and BLENKO. 1930s–1960s printed BLENKO HANDCRAFT as shown.

Steuben Glassworks

(est. New York, 1903, by Frederick Carder; acquired by Corning Glassworks, 1918).

Glossary

acid-etching technique for decorating or reducing ground by using acid to eat away areas unprotected by an acid-resist

acid-polishing process used to give a shiny finish by dipping glass into a mixture of hydrofluoric and sulphuric acid

ariel technique whereby air bubble designs are created by sand-blasting patterns onto a clear or multi-coloured blank in deep relief. This is then re-heated and cased in a layer of clear glass, trapping bubbles between the layers

aventurine from the Italian word for "chance"; decoration of flecked metallic particles

batch the mixture of molten glass in the pot

blank either a partially formed vessel to which further decorative techniques will be applied (such as "ariel" or "graal") or a standardized fully formed vessel to which another process (such as cutting) will be applied.

blowing iron long, hollow metal rod used to inflate the gather of glass

canes rods of glass drawn by the glass-blower to required thickness for use as decoration

cased pieces made of two or more layers of coloured glass or with coloured decoration sandwiched between two layers of clear glass

cutting deep cuts, either polished or matt, created by offering the piece to a stone wheel at various angles

diamond-point engraving minutely detailed, fine line decoration using a tool with a sharp diamond point

enamelling decorative technique in which coloured powdered glass suspended in an oily mixture is painted onto a piece and then fused by heating

engraving lightly abraded matt surface decoration created with a fine copper wheel

facet-cutting polished cutting, forming facets around an object

gather molten glass on the end of a blowing or pontil iron

graal a technique in which a small blank is cut, engraved or acid-etched to form a pattern. This is then re-heated, cased, and blown into the required form. The expanded pattern is trapped within the wall of the vessel

hand-blown free-blown glass whose shape is entirely formed through blowing and finishing on the pontil rod

intaglio a form of glass engraving executed using a small rotating stone wheel instead of a copper wheel, thereby producing deeper abrasions.

iridescence rainbow-like surface effect created with lustre colours or by exposing the piece to hot vapours of metal oxides

optical cutting glass cut and polished to optical quality, sometimes large areas, sometimes restricted to roundels

mitre cutting very deep, V-shaped cuts

mould-blowing method of blowing molten glass into a mould to produce both shape and pattern

pontil iron solid iron rod used to transfer the blown bubble of glass from the blowing iron for further shaping and/or finishing

pontil mark scar where the pontil iron or rod was removed from the base of a piece

pressed glass glass with a smooth interior and a moulded exterior made by being pressed into a mould by a plunger

pucella a glass-blowers tool with two metal-spring arms, used for shaping a vessel

refraction deflection of rays of light from a glass surface

sag bending flat glass, cut to shape, is placed over a concave cast iron mould, then both are put into a kiln and heated. When the glass has sagged into the mould, they are taken out and the glass is depressed using a convex cast iron plunger. Initially used by Chance Bros.

screen-printing glass decoration process in which ink is forced through a fine-mesh screen onto the glass surface.

star cutting multiple cuts meeting at a central point to create a star effect

studio glass one-off pieces designed and produced by artist-craftsmen

trailing thin threads of glass applied to the surface of a piece

wheel engraving decoration of a vessel by abrading its surface with a rotating copper wheel

wrythen spiral-twisted ribbed glass

Where to buy & see

One of the best places to start buying glass is from a specialist dealer, most of whom will be happy to share their knowledge and experience. Local auctions, antique fairs, and markets are also good sources of glass from this period, however, it is advisable to first develop your knowledge and confidence in the subject so you can distinguish between the enormous amount of glass on display. Museums offer an opportunity to look at and learn about major glass collections, and in addition to those listed below, many glass houses have their own museums, for instance: Barovier & Toso, Blenko, Daum, Iittala, Johansfors, Karhula, Kosta, Leerdam, Orrefors and Seguso.

GREAT BRITAIN
SPECIALIST DEALERS

Alfie's Antiques Market
13–25 Church Street
Marylebone
London NW8 8DT

Dave Mann & Mark Parrish
U.07 Stables Antique Market
m.parrish@ukgateway.net

Gary Grant
18 Arlington Way
London EC1R 1UY
www.choicepieces.com

Jeanette Hayhurst, Fine Glass
32a Kensington Church Street
London W8 4HA

Nigel Benson
20th Century Glass
58–60 Kensington Church Street
London W8 4DB
www.20thcentury-glass.com

Planet Bazaar
149 Drummond Street
London NW1 2PB
www.planetbazaar.co.uk

POST, Nick Jenkins
Units 33, 37 & 38
Stables Antique Market
www.postdesign.co.uk

Stables Antique Market
Chalk Farm Road
London NW1 8AH

The Ginnel Gallery
Antiques Centre
18–22 Lloyd Street
Manchester M2 5WA

Undercurrents
Twentieth Century Design
28 Cowper Street
London EC2A 4AS

www.FreeformsUK.com
58-60 Kensington Church Street
London W8 4DB

MUSEUMS

Brighton Art Gallery &
Museum
Church Street
Brighton BN1 1EE

British Museum
Great Russell Street
London WC1B 3DG

Broadfield House
Glass Museum
Compton Drive
Kingswinford
West Midlands DY6 9NS

Manchester City Art Gallery
Moseley Street
Manchester M2 3JL

Victoria and Albert Museum
Cromwell Road
London SW7 2RL

Turner Museum
Sheffield University
Sir Robert Hadfield Building
Mappin Street
Sheffield S1 3JD

CONTINENTAL EUROPE
SPECIALIST DEALERS

Harry & Isle de Haas
Postbus 15730
1001 NE Amsterdam
The Netherlands

Jacksons
Tyska Brinken 20
S-11127 Stockholm, Sweden

Loschs
Pfarrer-Jaegers-Str. 19
D.53909 Zuelpich, Germany

MUSEUMS

CA.RI.VE, Fondazione Casa di
Risparmio di Venezia
Palazzo Cavalli Franchetti
San Marco 2847
Venice, Italy

Finnish Glass Museum
Tehtaankatu 23
FIN-11910 Riihimaki, Finland

Musée de Verre
Quai du Maastricht 13,
B-4000 Liège, Belgium

Museum of Decorative Arts
Ul, 17 Listopadu
Prague 1, Czech Republic

Nationalmuseum
Södra Blasieholmshamnen
10324 Stockholm, Sweden

Smålands Museum
Södra Järnvägsgatan 2, Box 102
SE-351 04 Växjö, Sweden

**UNITED STATES
SPECIALIST DEALERS**

Lost City Arts
18 Cooper Square
New York NY 10003
www.lostcityarts.com

Gansvoort Gallery
72 Gansvoort Street
New York NY 10014

Galere
3733 South Dixie Highway
West Palm Beach
FL 33405

MUSEUMS

Corning Museum of Glass
1 Museum Way, Corning,
NY 14830-2253

Metropolitan Museum of Art
1000, 5th Ave, New York,
NY 10028-0198

What to read

**Andrews, F., Clarke, A.,
and Turner, I.** *Ysart Glass*, Volo
Editions (London, 1990)

Barovier Mentasti, R. *Venetian
Glass 1890-1980*, Arsenale Editrice
(Venice, 1992)

Beard, G. *Modern Glass*, Studio
Vista (London, 1968)

**Chamberlain, Rayner &
Stapleton** *Austerity to Affluence -
British Art & Design 1945-1962*,
Merrell Holberton (London 1997)

Cooke, F. *Glass - Twentieth Century
Design*, Bell and Hyman (London
1986)

Dawson, J. *Finnish Post-War Glass
1945-1996*, University of
Sunderland 1996

Deboni, F. and Klein, D. *Venini
Glass*, Umberto Allemandi
(Verona, c.1996)

Duncan, A. *Orrefors Glass*,
Antique Collectors Club
(Woodbridge, 1995)

Eige, E. & Wilson, R. *Blenko
Glass 1930-1953*, Antique
Publications (Ohio 1987)

**Evans, W., Ross, C., and
Werner, A.** *Whitefriars Glass:
James Powell & Sons of London*,
Museum of London (London,
1985)

Flavell, R. & Smale, C. Studio
Glassmaking, *Van Nostrand
Reinhold & Co.* (New York 1974)

Jackson, L. *The New Look -
Design in the Fifties*, Thames &
Hudson (London 1991)

Jackson, L. *Twentieth Century
Factory Glass*, Mitchell Beazley
(London 2000)

Jackson, L., ed. *Whitefriars Glass:
The Art of James Powell & Sons*,
Richard Dennis, Shepton
Beauchamp, (1996)

Klein, D. *Studio Glass SInce 1945 -
The Dan Klein Collection*, Royal
Pavillion (Brighton 1984)

Klein, D. & Lloyd, W. eds. *The
History of Glass*, Orbis (London
1984)

Opie, J. *Scandinavian Ceramics and
Glass in the Twentieth Century*, V&A
Museum (London 1989)

Petrona, S. & Olvie, J.L.
Bohemian Glass 1400-1989 (New
York 1990)

Polak, A. *Modern Glass*, Faber &
Faber (London, 1962)

Ricke, H. & Schmitt, E. *Italian
Glass Murano Milan 1930-1970*,
Prestel (Munich & New York
1997)

Ricke, H. and Thor, L., eds.
*Swedish Glass Factories, Production
Catalogues 1915-1960* Prestel
Verlag (Munich, 1987)

Stennett-Willson, R. *The Beauty
of Modern Glass*, Studio
(London, 1958)

Stennett-Willson, R. *Modern
Glass*, Studio Vista (London, 1975)

Steuben Crystal Steuben Glass
(New York 1956)

Index

Acknowledgements

The author would like to thank the following people for their help, information, encouragement and loaning of items for the book: Celia Bailey, Alex Bishop, Paul Bishop, Graham Cooley, Roger Dodsworth, Jan Eaton, Christina Glover, Gary Grant, Marcus Grey, Ina Harris, Kevin Harris, Jeanette Hayhurst, Deborah Jefferis, Nick Jenkins, Dave Mann, Virginia McLeod, Anne Metcalfe, Judith Miller, Mark Parrish, Tim Paterson, Anna Sanderson, Maureen Silverman, Steve Tanner.

All pictures photgraphed by Steve Tanner for Octopus Publishing Group Ltd, courtesy of Nigel Benson, except: **21tl, 31br** Christie's Images; **6bl, 31br, 53tr** Octopus Publishing Group Ltd/Tim Ridley/Planet Bazaar; **35bc** Octopus Publishing Group Ltd/Tim Ridley/Boom!; **6tr, 45tc** Miller's Publications/Christie's South Kensington; **53br** Octopus Publishing Group Ltd/Tim Ridley/Target Gallery; **54br** Octopus Publishing Group Ltd; **Jacket photograph** Octopus Publishing Group Ltd/Steve Tanner/Nigel Benson.